G000122835

ASPECTS OF
THE YORKSHIRE COAST 2

Aspects
of the
Yorkshire Coast
Discovering Local History

2

Edited by
ALAN WHITWORTH

Series Editor
Brian Elliott

Wharncliffe Books

First Published in 2000 by
Wharncliffe Books
an imprint of
Pen and Sword Books Limited,
47 Church Street, Barnsley,
South Yorkshire. S70 2AS

Copyright © Wharncliffe Books 2000

For up-to-date information on other titles produced under the
Wharncliffe imprint, please telephone or write to:

> **Wharncliffe Books**
> **FREEPOST**
> **47 Church Street**
> **Barnsley**
> **South Yorkshire S70 2BR**
> **Telephone (24 hours): 01226 - 734555**

ISBN: 1-871647-79-7

All rights reserved. No part of this publication may be
reproduced, stored in a retrieval system, or transmitted, in
any form or by any means, electronic, mechanical,
photocopying, recording or otherwise, without the prior
permission in writing of the publishers.

This book is sold subject to the condition that it shall not,
by way of trade or otherwise, be lent, resold, hired out or
otherwise circulated without the publisher's prior consent in
any form of binding or cover other than that in which it is
published and without a similar condition including this
condition being imposed on the subsequent purchaser.

A CIP catalogue record of this book is available from the
British Library

Cover illustration: Scarborough, North Bay in the nineteenth century,
showing the harbour and lighthouse.

Printed in Great Britain by
Redwood Books, Trowbridge, Wiltshire

CONTENTS

INTRODUCTION

---

by Alan Whitworth

VARIETY IS THE SPICE OF LIFE, and in this second volume of
Aspects of the Yorkshire Coast, there is a plentiful diversity of material - from tales of an Indian Prince to a look at Holy Wells. The success
of the acclaimed 'Aspects' series is based upon a simple but proven
formula: local and family history is such a popular interest that a
collection of well-researched and well-written articles by both experi-
enced and new writers, relating to a single town and surrounding area
or to an identifiable geographical district, will appeal to a wide read-
ership. In this respect Wharncliffe Publishing have fully embraced the
concept in an attractively presented and well illustrated format which
does not compromise on the quality of production whilst its editors
always have an eye on maintaining an appropriate standard.

The 'Aspects' series was founded in 1993 with the publication of
Aspects of Barnsley, edited by Brian Elliott, which was so successful
that it has now reached six volumes. Under Melvyn Jones's editorship,
Aspects of Rotherham appeared in 1995, and this too has seen a number
of volumes published annually. Later, the series was extended to
Doncaster, Sheffield, Leeds, Huddersfield, Wakefield and Bradford
among the most recently published titles, and then over the borders
into Lancashire and elsewhere around the country.

In this volume of *Aspects of the Yorkshire Coast*, various areas of the
East Coast fishing industry are rightly given prominence. The sea, of
course, is a prime factor in determining the pattern of industry hereabouts. and plays a crucial role in the shaping of the people and the
communities.

By contrast, a little hitherto known aspect of maritime life is revealed
in Ben Chapman's brief article of the Cloughton whales, a number of
which, no doubt along with many unrecorded leviathans, have become
stranded and died on the coast of East Yorkshire from Whitby to the
Humber Peninsula.

Continuing the nautical theme, Peter Howorth presents a graphic
description of the smuggler's in a small village on the outskirts of
Scarborough, which is today a respectable suburb of that place, and
whose prospects today belie the rioting and illicit goings-on that
occurred over several months, and whose effects even reached

England's capital city, London.

Dr Andrew White, whose family goes back two hundred years in Whitby history, has written eloquently on the Victorian aspects of this seaside town, tracing its resurgence and growth from the end of the Georgian period when Whitby went into a steep decline and was in danger of loosing its way as a significant community on the Yorkshire coast.

The rise and fall and rise of Bridlington is likewise charted in the article by Howard Peach who looks at its growth from the humble fishing hamlet of *Bretlington* to a major holiday resort and hoping to remain so in the twenty-first century.

Lastly, no Aspects volume would be complete without some reference to family history or biography. 'Plain Tales from Scalby' looks at the life of one family over three generations who were brought up and born in this pretty suburb village of Scarborough. Bound up with service in the Rowntree family, they recorded many of their doings in a journal and a number of letters and postcards survive, written between a later member of the Kidd family and a daughter of John W Rowntree, the Quaker cocoa magnate and social reformer. Then Alex Heywood has written a fine piece on the life of Andrew Marvell, the seventeenth century poet of Oliver Cromwell born on the East Coast.

Finally, this volume could not have been produced without the assistance of a fine team of 'backroom' staff at Wharncliffe Publishing, and mention should be made of the following individuals. On the production side Roni and Paul Wilkinson, father and son, who have made my task as editor a lot easier and therefore deserve my sincere thanks. I would also like to thank all at Wharncliffe involved in the promotion support services including Chief Executive, Mr Charles Hewitt and Mike Parsons, and finally Brian Elliott overall Series Editor for his invaluable contribution in keeping the work on track. In conclusion I should like to end this catalogue of thanks by expressing my appreciation to all the contributors who have given their time and talent and produced some excellent articles that will hopefully inspire others to research aspects of the Yorkshire coast for the benefit of future generations.

1. Bridlington – The Growth of a Holiday Resort

by Howard Peach

THIS MOST FAVOURED SHELTERED POSITION to the south of Flamborough Head must have been a strong inducement to early settlers. Roman coins have been unearthed on the beach, where a minor port, 'Safehaven Bay' developed. In Anglo-Saxon times here was 'Berhtel's farmstead', transmuted to 'Bretlington' in the Domesday Survey of 1086. Here, in later centuries was the nucleus of a small community known as the 'Quay' (Figure 1).

The first significant new departure was the foundation of an Augustinian Priory by Walter de Gant, Lord of the Manor, begun about the year 1113. Around it arose a second community, the 'Old Town', a little distance from the sea (allowing for centuries of erosion), and with long-lasting flexibility about its name – 'Bretlington' and 'Burlington' were but two of many variations. By 1200, however, it was well established enough to be granted a market and fair on Church Green. Like many Yorkshire monastic institutions the Priory prospered on sheep, and was soon exporting wool to

Figure 1. A detail of Thomas Jeffrey's map of 1772 showing the two distinct places of Bridlington and Bridlington Quay

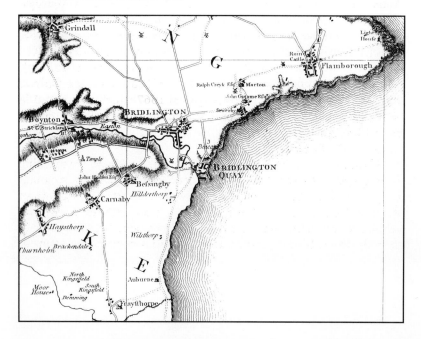

Flanders in its own ships. But fame and respect were won through Prior John (1320-79), an inspirational leader who was canonised in 1401. Thus, 'Burlington' acquired its own saint, whose shrine behind the high altar duly attracted steady streams of pilgrims, not perhaps on the scale of those who journeyed to Canterbury to see the tomb of Thomas-a-Becket, but, coincidence or not, in *The Canterbury Tales* Chaucer's character the Shipman knew Hull, and the Summoner began his story with the words:

> *Lordinges, ther is in Yorkshire, as I gesse*
> *A mersshy contree called Holderness...*

Such was the reputation of St John of Bridlington that following his victory at Agincourt (1415) King Henry V visited the shrine here to give public thanks.

It was another King Henry, unfortunately, who in 1537 ordered the destruction of the priory as part of an overall aim to suppress the monasteries and establish himself as supreme head of the Church of England. Anxious to divorce his Catholic queen, Catherine of Aragon, Henry VIII would brook no interference from the Pope. Moreover, the monasteries would provide much wealth for shoring up his defences such as those at Hull. The resultant protest, called the 'Pilgrimage of Grace' was ruthlessly put down and Prior William Wood of Bridlington was executed for his part in the uprising. Stone from the Priory was trundled down to the Quay for urgent repairs to the piers.

After the demolition of the Priory (except for the church of St Mary and the Bayle gatehouse), the Quay gained in strategic importance. On 20 February 1643, Queen Henrietta Maria, bringing arms from Holland to her beleaguered husband King Charles I, was obliged to land there, escaping Roundhead gunfire only by cowering in a ditch. In the year 1666, during a war with Holland, the little town was bombarded by Dutch warships. Despite this and other setbacks like the plague in 1667 which reappeared in 1721, trade expanded, coal coming in from Newcastle and timber from Scandinavia, while corn, barley, malt and local ale were despatched to London in the main.

Meantime, a civil contract of 1636 was to have far-reaching consequences. By the 'Great Town Deed' of that year and payment of £3260 to the Crown, Bridlington was taken over by a group of thirteen local men, the Lords Feoffees, who were to control all administrative affairs until the Local Government Board succeeded them in 1863. Indeed, certain responsibilities remain with them to this day. With stability and continuity guaranteed, during the eighteenth century the High Street and Westgate areas of the Old Town witnessed the building of many prestigious residences for professional men like doctors, lawyers, and merchants. Simultaneously but separately, the Quay needed and became home to many practical persons – boatmen, tidesmen, handlers of merchandise, and coastguards.

Commerce was not its only attraction, however, the golden beaches hereabouts began to be noticed. On his northern tour of 1769 Arthur Young commented on the bathing at Bridlington. Sailors coming ashore liked to enjoy themselves here, and one incident in particular relating to these, stands out in the town's history of this period. On 7 July 1785, Prince William Henry, Duke of Clarence, the future King William IV, the 'Sailor King', whilst a midshipman on the *Royal George* stayed at the *Ship Inn* in Prince Street. One can only speculate on the circumstances, but His Royal Highness had his face slapped by a chambermaid, Sally Gibson, clearly a proud, no-nonsense East Yorkshire lass!

Gradually the Quay became fashionable, and respectable. The Reverend John Wesley visited several times in the seventies and eighties. A wealthy Beverley man, John Courtney returned each year between 1788 and 1804, noting with interest the card players, the dancers, the tea drinkers and the strollers. Anna Seward, the so-called 'Swan of Lichfield', sentimental novelist and social observer came in 1793, writing in admiration of 'a boarded pier, one hundred and twenty yards in length and on which nine people may walk abreast... an admirable public walk' (Figure 2). She also noted, 'several families of consequence are at this place'. They could well have included Sir Christopher Sykes, second baronet of Sledmere,

Figure 2. The North Pier about 1800 when it was still constructed largely of wood.

who frequently left his estate to while away a few days at his Hilderthorpe retreat.

Curiously, it was a working man, James Coates who produced Bridlington's first official guide in 1805, which he wrote in rhyme. Something of its light, informative but unmistakable tongue-in-cheek flavour may be gleaned from the following extract:

> *In rich assemblage here delight*
> *The convalescent and polite.*
> *Peers, knights and squires and dames repair*
> *To bathe, and drink and take the air.*
> *Such situation on the coast*
> *Such air, such water none can boast.*[1]

The growing town could now reasonably claim to be a resort, advertising hot and cold baths, bathing machines, billiards, cards, dancing, together with the attractions of a safe beach with virtually no tidal hazards.

More aristocratic names soon featured in the Visitors List printed in the local newspaper. The year 1808 saw the patronage of the Duke and Duchess of Leeds and the Earl and Countess Fitzwilliam. Ordinary mortals, too, were finding their way to the town. By 1813 there were over seventy lodging houses to accommodate the visitors, swollen ten years later to more than a hundred.

For a time, progress appeared to be consolidatory rather than spectacular. The holiday base was still the Quay, with comparatively few excursionists making the short walk up St John's Street to the still separate Old Town. From 1833 gas lighting lent a romantic aura to the streets by night and encouraged later closing hours for card parties and entertainment during a season that was now established from mid-June to early October. A museum was started in 1834 and the following year an Agricultural Show promised a further annual delight.

Visitor numbers reached the one thousand mark in August 1838, some having travelled appreciable distances. Charlotte Brontë came the next year, by train from Leeds to Selby and thereafter by coach and gig. In her letters home she described people parading on the small North Pier but was less impressed by the noise from the 'Ranters Chapel'. Some readers have surmised that the fictitious 'Bretton' in her novel *Villette* might have been drawn from her visit to Bridlington.

Other grandees continued to frequent the town. In 1842 the Duke of Norfolk and family visited; and, interestingly, Admiral Sir Charles

Richardson stayed at the *Britannia*, formerly the *Ship Inn* favoured earlier by HRH the 'Sailor King'.

With so many visitors to the resort, leisure amenities sprang up and continued to flourish. A brass band played on an afternoon or evening; and 'Bishop's Improved Sea-Water Baths' on the Esplanade offered the more timorous souls an alternative to stepping on sand and pebbles. After considerable difficulties the North Pier, admired by Charlotte Brontë, was completed in 1843; and with the addition of a new South Pier in 1848 a more impressive harbour was created, soon filling with fishing boats and a variety of small craft and sailing ships (Figure 3). This ever-changing scene became a central attraction.

From 1846 it was only a few steps from the North Pier to the Victoria Rooms, built in Tudor-style and with a distinctive castellated tower. Immediately this became the social mecca for concerts, dancing, billiards, serious theatre and local dramatic productions; and here were situated the library and reading rooms. Before the end of the year the rather cumbersomely titled *Burlington Reporter and Burlington Quay Fashionable Advertiser* carried a report on what was to transform the country – the railway had arrived. At one o'clock in the afternoon of 6 October some two thousand excited people including the Lords Feoffees and the 'Railway King' himself, George Hudson (Figure 4), gathered to welcome from Hull the first three trains pulling sixty-six crowded carriages. The following year the railway line was extended to Filey and Scarborough.

Suddenly and dramatically the stagecoach era had finished, and famous and eagerly looked for vehicles disappeared from the roads – the 'British Queen' to the Quay, the 'Wellington' via Driffield to the

Figure 3. Bridlington harbour in the nineteenth-century with the paddle steamer Scarborough.

Old Town, both arriving from Hull; and the 'Tally-ho' which rumbled between the *Britannia Inn* and York.

The siting of the railway station just to the west of Quay Road and linking up with St John's Street and the Old Town had the eventual effect of drawing the two communities together, a process that became more apparent during the mid-nineteenth century with the development of new streets within the area.

Rail travel had a direct and dynamic impact on Bridlington as a holiday resort. Day excursions priced cheaply brought trainloads of folk from the West Riding and the North Midlands, especially from the colliery districts. Within a few years annual crowds estimated at up to five thousand in number converged on the August Bank Holiday beaches, but not without a whisper of criticism from the townspeople on the

Figure 4. George Hudson, the 'Railway King' as a young man. It was he who brought the railway to Bridlington which continued its prosperity.

unaccustomed manners and raucous vulgarity. A more restrained commercial view of around the year 1858 was that 'Bridlington attracts numbers of that class of visitor for whom Hornsea is too quiet and Scarborough too gay',[2] anticipating neatly the late Sir Nikolaus Pevsner's assessment over a century later, of 'a seaside resort neither as noisy as Blackpool or Southend nor as self-respecting as Filey'.[3] A few beach entertainers were trying their hand – a Punch and Judy man and the occasional minstrel group with blackened faces – but their day was not yet.

By the 1860s Bridlington was the place to be, and by self-aware middle class families, the place to be seen. A new hotel, built in 1866, was the *Alexandra* on the north end of the Promenade, which was to symbolise prestige for over a century. Hotels and lodging houses now totalled almost two hundred and thirty. The remarkable Sheffield team of architect Joseph Earnshaw and builder G W Travis, was putting up not only four-storey lodging houses behind the north promenade, but by 1869 had created such architectural gems as the Crescent and Marlborough Terrace.

The year 1866 was memorable too, for the completion of the Sea Wall Parade that extended sea defences beyond the north pier. In 1888 it was renamed the Royal Princes Parade and opened by HRH Albert Victor, eldest son of the Prince of Wales.

Many forms of entertainment now became established that for numerous visitors became the essence of a Bridlington holiday.

Horse-riding on the beach (Figure 5), tried in previous years but abandoned as perhaps too dangerous, was replaced by donkey rides, marshalled for several decades by Mrs Mary Knaggs. Punch and Judy became a permanent summer feature. Strolling or promenading as the band played became a new art form for ladies, and escorts, of sophisticated tastes. Sunday mornings on the Parade provided social opportunities for displaying finery and formal dress. For the slightly more adventurous, there had been for many years, omnibus excursions to Flamborough to see the cliffs and two lighthouses. Such trips were given a boost in the 1880s by the publication of RD Blackmore entitled *Mary Anerley*, a saga of local smugglers and the exploits and alleged cave of the redoubtable Robin Lythe. A little further up the coasts at Bempton were the 'climmers' – intrepid local men who were lowered over the cliff edge to collect the eggs of nesting sea birds, a practice not outlawed until 1954.

In the following decade came the Pierrots, entertainers dressed at first like clowns, with white caps and big black buttons, who performed songs, sketches, dances and comic turns on the beach, or as part of a carefully rehearsed street theatre. First appearing in 1892 and continuing until the First World War were the trend-setting troupe named *Waterloo* (Figure 6), early striped blazers, straw boaters and black faces soon giving way to pantaloons, pompoms and ruffles. Another celebrated Edwardian troupe was Catlin's Royal Pierrots.

So began a period of prodigious innovation and variety. Entertainment proliferated with acrobats, fire-eaters, performing dogs and bears, and hurdy-gurdy men with barrel organs. The brass band caught popular enthusiasm, and in particular, the 'Railway Porters' under their conductor William Whiting, himself a porter. They undertook their early practices in the station waiting room. A

Figure 5. Galloping Snobs by the Seaside, a cartoon from Punch showing the dangers from this activity and highlighting the total disregard that 'High Society' had over the lower classes.

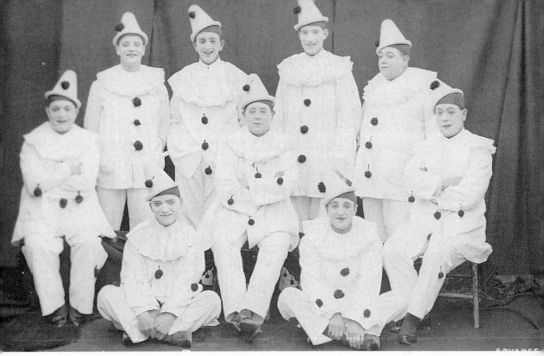

Figure 6. The Waterloo Pierrots in 1911

tremendous fillip to evening concerts was the introduction of electric lighting from 1890, Princes Parade being among the first streets to be lit (Figure 7). A Hydro opened on South Marine Drive; and a switchback railway, charging two pence a ride was constructed near the seaward end of Sands Lane. This lasted until 1912.

Bright new shops set up, selling clothes, beach toys and accessories, souvenirs and confectionery. An entrepreneur who came to have many imitators was George Gibbins who ran a lively rock-making emporium in King Street between 1878 and 1914. Picture postcards requiring a half-penny postage stamp became readily and cheaply available for sending to family and friends left back home. At this period of Victoria's reign, the cards carried little to offend propriety and were mostly sedate views of the resort which in 1899 received a Charter of Incorporation, becoming a borough with mayor and corporation, and the indulgence of a coat of arms declaring the motto *Signum Salutis Semper* – Good Health Always. Bridlington had surely arrived!

From 1896 new centres of entertainment sprang up, the north side vying with the south. On Quay Road appeared the People's Palace, designed by Joseph Earnshaw, which had a concert hall capacity for holding an audience of a thousand persons and which also had a bowling-green. This was to become the prime domain of an illustrious corporation manager for many years, Charles Palmer, producer of concerts, dances, Pierrot shows and revues galore. Its

Figure 7. Holidaymakers strolling on Princes Parade about the year 1910.

rival on the south side, behind a strengthened sea wall, was the New Spa with theatre and promenades and a glass dome that soon became a minor landmark. The first resident orchestra was led by a German maestro, Herr Mayer Lutz, quickly to become a favourite in those carefree pre-war days. Although like so many public buildings in Bridlington, the New Spa was burnt down (Figure 8), in this instance in 1906, it was rebuilt the very next year.

The Edwardian era which followed Queen Victoria's death in 1901 was a high water mark in the town's popularity. To the string of existing entertainment halls were added in 1904 a splendid Floral Pavilion in Princes Parade, on the site of the former Bishop's Baths and open-air Bandstand. Here began the early career of boy singer Jack Hylton, later to be acclaimed as a concert pianist and all-round musician. More glories were to come. Within two years Bridlington witnessed its most magnificent occasion to date, involving a colourful

Figure 8. The Spa Theatre, Bridlington after the fire of 20 October 1906.

procession stretching for five miles. On 6 July 1906, Sir W Vaughan Morgan, Lord Mayor of London, performed the opening ceremonies of the new Sea Walks, Victoria Terraces and the Grand Pavilion. Here, until the disastrous fire of 1935 that destroyed it, many future celebrities were to make their debut at the Grand Pavilion, including dancers like Maud Allen and the male quintet, the 'Beaconsfield Singers'.

A 'first' for the town, begun in 1907, was the creation of the eye-catching Floral Clock, lovingly planted in the garden of the New Pavilion. The colourful twelve-foot dial was painstakingly built up from hundreds of plants and became a regular place of pilgrimage for all age groups. Later a floral staircase and a topiary bear were added.

Attractive too, were the mobile bathing huts available from a new generation of the Bishop family. The shire horses of Mr Bishop drew the huts into a foot or two of sea-water, and his wife assisted the ladies to descend the steps into the foaming surf. Those were decorous days!

Meanwhile, Bridlington was becoming a desirable place to settle and live in. Enjoying easy train rides to and from their offices, Hull businessmen bought properties in relaxed and often picturesque environs. By 1914 the town's resident population had risen to fifteen thousand; and there were more than nine hundred boarding houses, inns, etc to cater for the enormous influx of visitors each summer. Interestingly, this number declined to some seven hundred in 1921.

Nevertheless, whatever the reason for the reduction in the number of boarding house, inns etc., the inter-war years were another boom period in Bridlington's history. Opening on 15 July 1926, the Spa Royal Hall was badly damaged by fire in 1932, but re-emerged on the same foundations to admit an admiring public yet again on 30 July of that same year (Figure 9). The premises included a Palm

Figure 9. Royal Hall, Bridlington in September 1939.

Court and Solarium, and the largest dance floor in the north of England. Up until 1939 the star resident attraction was the genial Herman Darewski and his famous radio band. Darewski Dances and Jolly Nights, his compositions like *K-K-K-Katie* and *In the Twi-light*, and his occasional stunts, like collecting roses to build a huge bouquet, made him a legendary figure in the town. When Darewski was resting, the Spa became the venue of galas, fireworks, operas, carnivals and vaudeville shows (Figure 10). Outside there was another royal occasion in September 1928 with the opening of the Princess Mary Promenade.

An innovation of long-term significance was the erection of 'Fun City' on Marine Drive in 1921. Its array of automatic machines, pintables, shooting galleries, dodgems, organ grinders, and so forth, aimed at the younger visitor, was visibly to alter the character of sea-front allurements. The idea of the amusement arcade, controversial in some quarters, caught on, and by 1939 there were seven huge arcades offering similar facilities, and included the Palladium Amusements on Prince Street and Joyland on the Promenade.

During the later years of the 1920s and early 1930s a musical entertainment manager called Alfred Barker brought many national luminaries to the Promenade scene. Fred Rayne's concert party became celebrated as radio's North Regionals, wherein a young and ambitious actress named Beryl Reid began to make a reputation for herself.

Success brought about expansion and change. The old Grand Pavilion having outlived its popularity was demolished in 1936. The site was opened up and a new Grand Pavilion arose in Victoria Terrace Gardens (Figure 11). Never quite rivalling the New Spa, it provided however, an alternative dance hall, theatre, and venue for musicals, summer revues and concert parties. A new venture in hotels came with the opening in March 1937 of the Expanse on North Marine Drive. Its five-storeys and thirty-eight bedrooms set new standards and fashions in luxurious accommodation aimed at the more select range of summer visitors.

Whatever their social origins, nearly all visitors came to view the sea and to stroll along the 'Proms' and piers. The beach at Bridlington offered beautiful sands, safe bathing, donkey rides and deck chairs by the thousand (Figure 12). On the south side of

Figure 10. An advert for the Spa Royal Hall entertainments in 1947.

SPA ROYAL HALL
Manager for the Corporation : ARTHUR W. ALLCOCK

'Hello! Children'

Commencing 5th July, 1947, and daily at 2-30 p.m. throughout the Season
(Thursdays Excepted)

BRIDLINGTON'S OWN CHILDREN'S ENTERTAINMENT

featuring

ERNEST SEWELL
UNDER ROYAL PATRONAGE

The Children's Star Entertainer.

CONJURING, VENTRILOQUISM, DANCING, LIVING MARIONETTES, COMPETITIONS, ETC.

Ernest Sewell
has had the honour of presenting his entertainment on eleven occasions before Members of the Royal Family, and has appeared at Windsor Castle and Buckingham Palace on eight occasions.

Figure 11. The new Grand Pavillioon

the harbour was the chance to watch the fishing boats unload their catch, and perhaps have a photograph taken alongside a huge halibut or even the occasional basking shark. Organised fishing parties were on offer. An interest in fishing gave rise to an annual sea-angling festival that was well supported from its beginnings in 1922. Scottish 'drifters' and herring boats were so numerous at this time that it was claimed that any sure-footed person could walk from the South Pier to Crane Wharf (parallel to the North Pier) without getting wet feet.

From the mid-nineteenth century paddle steamers had come in from Scarborough to take visitors on short sea trips (Figure 13). Famous among those in Bridlington harbour was the black and white twin-screw steamer the *Yorkshireman*, arriving in 1928 for the first time and remaining in service until about 1955. This replaced another very popular craft the *Frenchman,* originally a paddle tug.

Another well-supported annual nautical event organised by the Royal Yorkshire Yacht Club was the Regatta and Aquatic Sports. Indeed, the Regatta still continues. In those days, however, the daring nightly dive off the North Pier at high tide by the 'Houdini of the Water', Professor Gautier, drew vast expectant crowds. By day the professor ran bathing events in the Queen's Square Swimming Baths.

Fortunately, Gautier never needed the services of the lifeboat, whose exploits have captured the imagination of generations. Still talked of is the 'Great Gale' of 10 February 1871, when even the lifeboat *Harbinger* was overturned after several rescue attempts. Six crew member's perished that day and seventy more from thirty wrecked and damaged vessels. Some found a resting-place in the Priory churchyard, which until about 1970 provided the setting for the annual Fisherman's Sunday Memorial Service.

For many, part of the magic of Bridlington lies in its numerous fascinating historical connections. Who could ever have thought that

Lawrence of Arabia would finish his Service career as ordinary airman TE Shaw, working as an RAF speedboat mechanic on inshore craft, and lodging at the *Ozone Hotel*. Only a few months after leaving Gummers Wharf for the final time in 1935, Lawrence was killed in a motor cycle accident. Today his name is recalled in the 'Lawrence Complex' and in the simple sundial situated in the South Cliff Gardens opposite.

During the last years of the 1930s, Lawrence's final sphere of operations was excitedly pointed out by knowledgeable trippers, some of whom would be likely to walk or take the miniature train along the beautiful cliff tops to Sewerby. Standing prominently in fine landscaped grounds, the Hall passed from private hands into municipal and was opened to the public on 1 June 1936, by Amy Johnson, the Hull-born girl who had made history by her solo flights to Australia and South Africa. Her flying suits, log books, awards and memorabilia still form the focus of the museum collection there.

During the Second World War, Bridlington acquired a reputation as the 'Dover of the North', its holiday trade suffering severe dislocation. Amongst the direct casualties were the Electricity Showrooms and houses next door (Figure 14), General Post Office, the People's Palace, Queen's Square Baths, the Britannia Hotel and much property in Hilderthorpe Road. Also the harbour, with its RAF Maritime Rescue Unit, was frequently attacked by the enemy. During the hostilities, music and entertainment had been the key factors in keeping up national morale, and it was vital that star

Figure 12. The sands of Bridlington, enjoyed by young and old.

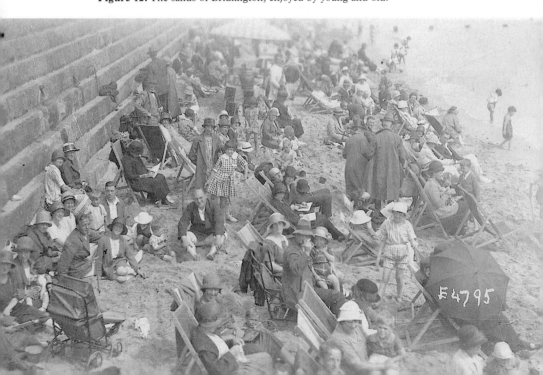

entertainers should set the highest standards in an uncertain post-war era. The 1946 summer season saw Harry Benet's Gaiety Fayre at the Grand Pavilion, with lavish sets and costumes. Household names for many years were 'The Brothers in Harmony', Ceres and Edwin Harper at the Spa Royal Hall (Figure 15), although each went on independently to become a musical director, Edwin Harper working into his seventieth year.

It was becoming clear after the war years, however, that traditional ideas about the annual seaside holiday were under threat. Day-trippers and weekenders still flooded in to the resort during the summer, but fewer visitors were staying for more than a week. Boarding houses began to feel the pinch as self-catering accommodation developed, together with various forms of camping. By 1953 some four thousand holidaymakers were encamped in seven caravan and other sites including Butlin's. The South Cliff Camp site mushroomed railway carriages, shacks and bungalows, old buses and ex-army huts. Further south at Wilsthorpe, the Holiday Village grew increasingly popular. Modes of travel changed too. By the late-1960s over half of holiday arrivals were by motor-car.

There were other worrying trends. According to a 'Holidaymakers Survey' in 1973, conducted by the Junior Chamber of Commerce, some seventy per cent of visitors were over forty-five, with the 20s and 30s age group in serious decline as resort visitors. Younger people were travelling to more distant climes in search of sun and fun as the price of package holidays abroad fell. A symptom of these changing times was the demolition of the *Alexandra Hotel* in 1975, whose site was covered with luxury flats.

Yet there is much to commend in the town, and the Corporation has done its best to promote these aspects. Floral decorations, for example, were taken seriously and the Parks and Gardens Department showed a great deal of imagination in this area, so much so, that in 1973 Bridlington was joint winner of the national 'Britain in Bloom' contest, and was many times Area finalist. Top show-business names continued to appear on the bill at the Floral Pavilion and particularly frequented the Spa Royal Hall. Cinemas, night-clubs, pubs, disco dance halls and bingo houses all did well during the season, as did the sea-front amusement arcades. Harbour trips, however, were less buoyant. Pleasure steamers were fewer, but old favourites like the *Yorkshire Belle*, the *Britannia* and the *Flamborian* (previously named the *Boys Own*) still monopolised the trade.

Yet the 1980s brought no respite from the general downward trend, and the resort continued to decline. On the site of the former

The Harbour, Bridlington

Figure 13. Bridlington Harbour in the twentieth century with the paddle-steamers alongside the pier.

Figure 14. The remains of the Electricity Showrooms and the house next door in Quay Road after bombardment in the Second World War. Alan Whitworth

Grand Pavilion, however, was built the huge 'Leisure World' complex, opened on 3 April 1987, by HRH the Duchess of Kent, and costing £4.8 million. With Bridlington still largely targeting the family market, facilities, aimed very much at providing interests for the younger generation, include water sports, wave pool, waterslides, fitness studio, sauna, solarium, tropical walks, disco, cabaret, theatre and exhibitions.

In some other respects, Bridlington's place in the vanguard of modern holiday destinations is less assured. The town's Assisted Area Status, granted in 1993, although important for its future, is hardly a winning line in the holiday brochure. A report, *Building a Better Bridlington* published three years later by a Regeneration Partnership of local professional people underlined a number of serious issues in the continued spiral of depression. However, on two recent enterprises, the warmest congratulations are due. In Bridge Street the Lords Feoffees have inaugurated the most marvellous museum, which while being up-to-date in its presentation, tells the story of the town's historic development under the title of *Beside the Seaside*. The present author gratefully and gladly acknowledges its inspirational value. The other project, in Cardigan Road, is the construction of the Emmanuel Church, surely the last word in modern ecclesiastical architecture which has risen Phoenix-like from the ashes of the former church that burnt down. This Church always seems to be active and available to resident and visitor alike and the kitchen kettle is generally hot!

Truly we live in changing times, and residents of Bridlington may have to accept that the good old days will never be fully recaptured. Amenities and appearances will always matter desperately (Figure 16). But for those who find the simplest of pleasures the most satisfying; the lure of the sea, that harbour, a haven for artists and fishermen, and the inviting beaches, all set against that incomparable curve of coastline up to Flamborough which first attracted

Figure 15. An advert for the Spa Royal Hall with Ceres Harper and his new Dance Orchestra

SPA ROYAL HALL
BRIDLINGTON
Manager for the Corporation   ·   ARTHUR W. ALLCOCK

SUMMER SEASON, 1947
Commencing
Whit Saturday, May 24th

Ceres Harper
AND HIS NEW
DANCE ORCHESTRA

FEATURING

"THE BROTHERS IN HARMONY"
(CERES AND EDWIN HARPER)
of B.B.C. Regular Broadcasts.

Thanks for the mem..or...y

DANCING   CABARET   CARNIVALS
SPECIAL FEATURE CONCERTS

STAR ATTRACTIONS EVERY SUNDAY
Throughout the Season

EASTER SUNDAY — APRIL 6th at 8
Eric Barker and Pearl Hackney
TWO FAMOUS STARS OF B.B.C. "MERRY-GO-ROUND."

The Premier Ballroom of the North with a delightfully sprung floor. Solariums. Palm Court. Open-air Sun Terrace. Café More than a quarter of a million patrons were entertained during the 1946 Summer Season.

Figure 16. Bridlington Harbour today overlooked by new flats which replaced the *Alexandra Hotel* in 1975.

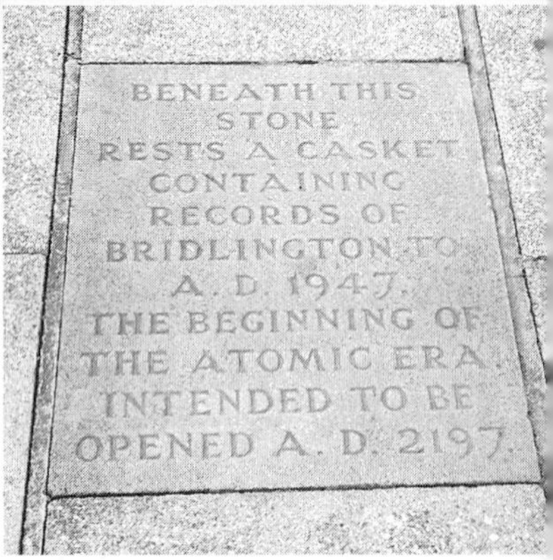

Figure 17. The time capsule buried for the enjoyment of future generations.

those early settlers; together or separately they will always bring the faithful back to 'Berhtel's farmstead'.

In conclusion, one futuristic observation (Figure 17). In the footpath leading to the front entrance of the Town Hall is a stone slab inscribed with the following words:

> *Beneath this stone rests a casket containing records of Bridlington to AD 1947, the beginning of the Atomic Era, intended to be opened AD 2197.*

It is a safe bet that no other seaside resort in these islands takes its forward planning so seriously!

Notes and References

1. Quoted by S T Thompson, *Bridlington Guide Books*, p 6, 1970.
2. Attributed to Walter White in his book *Yorkshire Tour:* see J Fairfax-Blakeborough, *Yorkshire - East Riding*, p134. Hale, 1951.
3. Pevsner, Sir Nikolaus, *Yorkshire:York and the East Riding*, p196. Penguin Books, 1972.

2. When Elephants Roamed the Streets of Whitby

by Alan Whitworth

The rocks by Moultgrave too, my glories forth to set,
Out of their crannied cliffs can give you perfect jett.
Drayton

JUST OVER ONE HUNDRED and fifty years ago the first Sikh to settle in Britain arrived. No ordinary member of his caste, however, his name was Dhuleep Singh, dubbed the 'Black Prince'. Prince Dhuleep Singh was the son of the Maharajah Ranjit Singh, ruler of the Indian state of Punjab.

As an eleven-year-old boy, Dhuleep Singh was forced to surrender rule of his late father's independent state on the northern border of India when it was annexed to the Empire by Britain in 1849, where for some years previous it had been in the grip of a power struggle for its control following the death of his father the Maharajah.

It was thanks to the efforts of his mother, Rani Jindan, that the young Dhuleep was proclaimed Maharajah on his fifth birthday. Six years later however, he suddenly found himself a prince without people.

The British moved into the Punjab and Dhuleep Singh was presented with a treaty that demanded he cede all power immediately. 'He shall resign for himself and his heirs all right and title to the sovereignty,' it read. 'All the property of the state shall be confiscated to the Honourable East India Company.'

Among the family and state property was the fabulous Koh-i-Nor diamond which also had to be surrendered as a condition of the treaty. The gem, also known as the Mountain of Light, is still considered by the Sikh religion as its most treasured relic. Today it forms the centrepiece of the state crown of the Queen Mother and is even now the subject of impassioned debate over its rightful home. Meanwhile, back in the nineteenth century, the young Maharajah reacted to the loss of his nation in a positive manner by starting a new life under the tuition of a Scottish surgeon appointed to the task.

Within months, Dhuleep Singh was speaking English, had

Figure 1. A nineteenth century engraving of Queen Victoria.

adopted a new hairstyle and, crucially, shed the shackles of his caste, even to the extent of making a cup of tea for himself!

By the age of thirteen, he had converted to Christianity and six years later he arrived in England. Both tall and handsome, and now educated, Prince Dhuleep Singh was an instant success at Queen Victoria's court and so taken with him, the Queen (Figure 1) ordered that the teenager be granted both money and a grand home for himself and his retinue, writing in support of this decision: 'As we have been in complete possession of his enormous and splendid kingdom, we should do everything to render the position of this interesting and amiable Prince as agreeable as possible.'

Unsure of where to set up home in his newly adopted country, the 'Black Prince' took up the lease of *Mulgrave Castle*, home of the Most Noble the Marquis of Normanby, and came to Whitby in May 1858, dipping into his handsome annuity of £40,000 a year from the British Government to pay the rent.

Mulgrave Castle was then unoccupied while its owner, the Marquis of Normanby was residing in London; and his son, a former treasurer of the Royal Household, was serving as Lieutenant Governor of Novia Scotia.

The original *Mulgrave Castle* had had a long and honourable ancestry stretching back to the fourteenth century, and the remains of this castle still exist. After its destruction by order of Parliament following the English Civil War, it is supposed that its days as a residence were over. However, there is something about the order of the House of Commons in 1647, that appears to imply that the destruction was not so thorough as in many other Yorkshire castles

Figure 2. *Mulgrave Castle*, near Whitby, as Prince Duleep Singh would have known it.

and the phrase 'works made since these troubles be slighted and dismantled,' obviously cannot refer to an older structure, and we are told, some parts continued to be used as habitation so late as the year 1830.

The present *Mulgrave Castle* (Figure 2), to which the young Maharajah came, was commenced by Lady Katherine, the third wife of John Sheffield, Third Earl of Mulgrave and Duke of Buckinghamshire and Mulgrave (1648-1720), on the site of a house formerly occupied by the Steward of the Manor, named Shipton. Lady Katherine, the widow of James Annesley, Third Earl of Anglesey, married the Earl in 1706 and died in the year 1743. They had two sons, and two daughters, all of whom died in infancy, and a son Edmund, born on 3 January 1716, who inherited his fathers estates and died unmarried on 30 October 1735, leaving all to his mother, Lady Katherine, who bequeathed them to her grandchild (by her first husband) Constantine Phipps, from whom the present holder of the title is descended.

Amongst the funeral effigies preserved in the Islip Chapel of Westminster Abbey are those of the above Duchess of Buckingham, Lady Katherine and her three-year-old son, the Marquis of Normanby.

The Duchess was a natural daughter of King James II, and could never forget her distinguished parentage. Horace Walpole said that she was 'more made with pride than any mercer's wife in Bedlam.' Interestingly, the effigy referred to above, was actually carried at her funeral and was probably the last so used.

Extensive alterations to Lady Katherine's building were made by successive holders of the title, but in particular, it is to Constantine John Phipps, Earl of Mulgrave in 1792, that we owe a debt for the present castellated form which possibly took the eye of the young Prince.

Prince Dhuleep Singh was an affable person, and mingled freely in Whitby society (Figure 3). The seaport itself, during the nineteenth century attracted many famous and notable personages, and was considered a rising watering hole, largely due to the efforts of George Hudson, the 'Railway King' who had taken an interest in this North Yorkshire resort, and built it up by bringing the railway into the place and establishing the West Cliff estate with the *Royal Hotel* and West Cliff Saloon to cater for the gentility that flocked to Whitby on the iron rails.

Among the annual visitors to Whitby in the nineteenth century was James Russell Lowell (1819-1891), the American poet and essayist and later, the American Minister to the Court of St James, appointed in 1880, which appointment coincided with Lowell's first visit to Whitby, and from that year until 1889 he spent a month or six weeks here every year. A tremendous letter writer, in August 1889, he wrote to a Mrs Leslie Stephen:

> *...This is my ninth year at Whitby, and the place loses none of its charm for me. It is better than Cornwall...Whitby is coming more and more into the currents of civilisation. We have a spasmodic theatre and an American circus that seems a fixture. Last year there was a delightful clown who really looked as if he couldn't help it, and was a wonderful tumbler too. How the children would have liked it! One other amusement is the Spa*

Figure 3. A silhoutte of the 'Black Prince'.

(Figure 4), *where there is a band of music bad enough to please the Shah. It is brilliantly lighted, and at night it is entertaining to sit above and watch the fashionable world laboriously diverting themselves by promenading to and fro in groups, like a village festival at the opera. The sea, of course, is as fine and irreconcilable as ever. Thank God, they cannot landscape-garden him...*

While the young Prince might not have had an ear for the best in music, nevertheless it is said that he had a generous heart and was well-disposed to enter into the local community. However, it is understood that he imposed an almost caste system among his staff on the Mulgrave estate, believing in the proper 'order' of things and was once greatly annoyed to discover a farm foreman cleaning out a stable, a task the Maharajah thought only fit for stable-hands.

Hunting was another favourite pastime of the young Prince. TH Whelan's, *History of the North Riding*, published in 1859, provides a rare glimpse of what must have been one the Maharajah's earliest hunting expeditions in the neighbourhood – a foray onto the moors near Ugthorpe.

While making our survey and gazing at the lovely views of the German Ocean (now named the North Sea) *we were enormously*

Figure 4. The West Cliff Saloon at Whitby, in the nineteenth century locally known as the Spa. *Alan Whitworth*

THE PAVILION.

aroused by a motley crew marching in line across the moors. In the centre was a fine stalwart man of some five and twenty summers, arrayed in gorgeous oriental dress – the Maharajah Dhuleep Singh. On either side of him were two swarthy sons of India, his Royal Falconers, with belled hawks on their shoulders, while six English gamekeepers in scarlet uniforms filled the picturesque tableau.

The Prince also inevitably, it appears, travelled north for 'the Season' and was often the guest of some Scottish laird, attending shooting parties with the nobility of England.

Never a recluse, in return, he also entertained often. The *Whitby Gazette* for Saturday, 10 September 1859, reported that 'the Most Noble the Marquis of Normanby arrived at Whitby by the mid-day train on Tuesday, and after visiting the Rt Honourable Lord Broughton, at the *Royal Hotel*, drove on to *Mulgrave Castle*, where he intended staying some time with His Highness the Maharajah Dhuleep Singh.'

In the first week of the New Year of 1860, the Prince held a party for the neighbourhood and staff, which many locals attended. The *Whitby Gazette* reported that

the scene was one of the grandest demonstrations which it has for some time been our province to record. The Sunday School scholars on the estate, numbering well on a hundred, were first treated with tea, in company with about the same number of clergy, gentry, and principal inhabitants of the district... As darkness veiled our earth the whole company passed from the castle... to the open air, to lose themselves in wonder and astonishment at the immense bonfires, and brilliant display of pyrotechnics... The view from the West Cliff was beautiful, and the effect pleasing...

This Sunday School New Year party, hosted by the Maharajah, became an annual event.

He also continued the tradition of allowing visitors during the summer months into the formal gardens of the estate and to view the romantic ruins of the original *Mulgrave Castle*, an annual tradition that is continued to this day. These open days the Prince advertised in the local newspaper.

At the end of 1860, the local newspaper reported that, 'His Highness Dhuleep Singh and Colonel Oliphant, left *Claridge's Hotel*, London, on Monday (December 11) for *Windsor Castle*, to visit Her Majesty, and returned the next day.' This was one of a number of invitations that the young Prince accepted, which he always made in the company of Colonel Oliphant who it seems was his secretary and mentor.

Sometime in 1863, Prince Dhuleep Singh purchased outright *Elveden Hall* in Suffolk, where he later took up residence. Its 17,000 acres, like the estate of Mulgrave, soon echoed to the calls of peacocks and elephants and it became a regular venue for Royal shooting parties headed by the Prince of Wales. But even though the Maharajah lived at Elveden for much longer than the four years he spent at Mulgrave, the impact that he and his extensive retinue made on the placid East Anglian countryside can scarcely have matched the stark incongruity of their excursions around the district of this isolated coastal resort.

The 'Black Prince' never forgot his time at Mulgrave, and indeed, he left an indelible imprint that still survives to this day and which is still of immense benefit to the neighbourhood and enjoyed by thousands each year. It was during his sojourn that he encountered an unforeseen problem. At that date, *Mulgrave Castle* was even more isolated from Whitby than today, as no road linked it to the town except a narrow track that climbed and twisted via the village of Dunsley nor was there any direct communication with Sandsend. Because of this visitors and residents usually travelled to Sandsend via the beach at low tide, or by boat when the tide was in. All deliveries too, had to be organised that way. Coal for instance, was brought by flat-bottomed 'cats' and beached on the sands nearby then carted to the castle.

Figure 5. The former toll-house along the Whitby-Sandsend Road as it is today. *Alan Whitworth*

It is also said, that the elephants of the Prince did not like the unaccustomed feel of sand between their toes. So the Maharajah went to the considerable trouble and expense of building a road from the castle to Whitby. The very first coast road in the district. Some say that this is fiction, however, and that the young Prince did not have elephants at Mulgrave.

What is true, is that Dhulep Singh did contribute financially to the building of a road. The 'Maharajah's Road' as it was known did not follow the present road, however, but crossed the golf course closer to the cliffs then the present highway. At Raithwaite ravine, near Sandsend, it looped inland to avoid the need for a large embankment or bridge. Only at the former toll-house, still standing today, do the old and new roads coincide. The road then continued along the present course of Upgang Lane to Flowergate Cross where it ran down into Flowergate.

If the tale of elephants roaming the streets of Whitby is a fabrication of the imagination, the Maharajah certainly had a string of fine horses that he often drove at a furious pace between Whitby and Sandsend.

The road was available to all, but at a cost, and a toll-house of sandstone was erected on the road side (Figure 5). This still stands

Figure 6. A selection of typical nineteenth century jet jewellery as might have been presented to the wife of Price Duleep Singh by the people of Whitby. *Alan Whitworth*

today, and while the road is now free of all tolls, the collection of dues continued for many years and the management of the road was once in the private ownership of the Pyman family, local shipowners. Interestingly, when the County Council replaced the Maharajah's road with a straighter link in 1925, the new highway was considered important enough to be opened by the then Minister of Transport.

For whatever purpose Prince Dhuleep's road was intended, the link was greatly welcomed by the district. The *Whitby Gazette* described it as 'this very important accommodation', and just before the road opened it prophesied, 'the drive to Mulgrave Castle, Sandsend and Lythe will thus be made one of the most delightful to be found on the sea coast of England.'

Although the new road was a considerable improvement to travel around the district, it was still not without its dangers. On Saturday, 22 October 1864, the *Whitby Gazette* reported the occurrence of '...a highway robbery on the new road between Upgang and East Row (Sandsend)...' when a youth was attacked and robbed of his meagre possessions.

In 1864, Dhuleep Singh married the seventeen-year-old daughter of a German missionary, Bamba Muller, who bore him three sons and three daughters – all of who were given English names and several of whom became Queen Victoria's godchildren and in 1993 a superb doll, complete with a huge wardrobe of outfits and exquisite accessories presented by Queen Victoria to one of their children, which had survived to the present day, was valued at between £10,000 and £15,000.

This gift was not the only one the young Prince and his family were to receive. Such was the esteem that the residents of Whitby felt for him, that in October 1864, it was reported in the local newspaper, that the Maharanee Bamba, bride of Dhuleep Singh, was presented with a selection of Whitby jet jewellery (Figure 6) '... in appreciation not only of his private character, but of the great benefits (enjoyed) by the Town during the residence of His Highness at Mulgrave Castle.'

As he grew older, however, the deposed Maharajah's playful decadence was replaced by a sobering realisation of what he had lost in his homeland. A trip back to the Punjab to bury his mother who had died in London in 1863 at *Abington House,* Kensington, began a spiral of depression and he continued to reflect on what might have been. His wife died in 1887 and he set the tongues of polite society wagging when he took up with a working-class London girl called Ada Wetherill.

After fathering two children by her, Prince Dhuleep travelled to Russia where he is said to have posed as an Irish rebel in an effort to persuade Czar Alexander III to invade India and restore him to the throne.

Unfortunately, this audacious plot, which involved the supposed raising of Irish troops against the British, was soon uncovered by Army intelligence. The Maharajah was subsequently arrested for treason and all his possessions confiscated. In 1893, at the age of fifty-five years old, His Highness the Maharajah Dhuleep Singh died penniless in Paris in exile, not only from his homeland of India, but from his adopted country, England.

Today, he is buried at Elveden, which over the years has become a place of pilgrimage for Sikhs. On the one-hundredth anniversary of Dhuleep Singh's death, it was decided to erect a lasting memorial to him in the form of a bronze statue which was finally put up and unveiled on a small wooded island in Thetford, in Norfolk, on Thursday, 29 July 1999, by HRH Prince Charles, witnessed by representatives of Britain's 500,000-strong Sikh community.

Harbinder Singh, director of the £100,000 statue appeal, said after the unveiling ceremony, 'This restores him to his rightful place in history. He has been neglected in the past and the Sikh community has not always been aware of his contribution (to their history).'

He symbolises Sikh sovereignty and the Sikh presence in this country. While it is true that Britain annexed the Punjab, we are trying to put a positive interpretation on history. What happened was well-documented and cannot be changed.

Prince Dhuleep Singh had left Mulgrave by 1864. On 19 December 1863, the sale of his farming stock was reported in the *Whitby Gazette*, where he was described as 'late of Mulgrave Castle'. Yet while his residence at Elveden, whose purchase was considered at the time a great extravagance, has overshadowed his time at Whitby, nevertheless hereabouts he is still remembered with affection and there are those whose parents recall their employment during his stay with pride.

3. Wells and Holy Wells of the Yorkshire Coast

by Edna Whelan

ANYONE WHO IS UNAWARE of one of our most ancient traditions may understandably ask, what is a Holy Well?

When we, today, think of a well, we imagine a deep hole in the ground containing fresh water with a stone parapet and a wooden framework above supporting a wooden roller. Using a handle to turn the roller allows a bucket attached to a chain or rope to be let down into the water to be filled up. This is not a Holy Well but a man-made artesian well and it is only comparatively recently in the long history of humankind that man has dug into the ground to find water. The name 'well' covers a much wider field and goes back thousands of years in time. It is described in the dictionary, in relationship to a spring, as being 'archaic.'

The definition of a Holy Well is that of a natural spring of water issuing from the ground of its own accord that never runs dry, and which also contains certain natural minerals that give the water particular healing properties. The water of a Holy Well is always crystal clear at its source and in order to differentiate it from other never failing springs it has been given a name.

A stone or brick trough has sometimes been set to catch and contain the water for a while and in many cases this trough has been covered by a small roofed structure of stone called a Well House.

Many different customs were once performed at the wells at certain times of the year, and some Holy Wells are still the focal point for pilgrimage (Figure 1). Because of their ancient origins and sanctity wells have, inevitably, acquired accompanying legends and folk stories.

Figure 1. *Coffin Well*, Tissington, Derbyshire. Well Dressing was once common to wells throughout England, but today is confined almost exclusively to the county of Derbyshire, where many village wells are still traditionally 'blessed' and dressed with flowers, and then visited by thousands. *Alan Whitworth*

Figure 2. Hinderwell, St Hilda's Well in the nineteenth century before restoration in 1912.

A few of the Holy Wells have retained all of these requirements but sadly, many have been lost with the passage of time.

St Hilda's Well at Hinderwell village, along the East Coast and just north of Whitby, is one of my favourite Holy Wells and is one of the Sacred Springs which has still preserved all of its properties. It can be found within the churchyard, after descending a rough flight of steps, and is covered by a small sturdy well-house (Figure 2). As it states on a carved stone above the water 'this well was restored by Hilda Palmer in the Year 1912.' All that was here previously to this date to catch the water was a stone trough.

The water at Hinderwell is certainly crystal clear and it is reputedly beneficial for the curing of sore eyes and for the removal of warts by bathing the affected parts in the water.

It was once the custom, on Ascension Day, to fill a bottle with water from the well and to add a small stick of liquorice and then to shake the bottle vigorously. This produced a thick brown liquid that made a delicious drink. The same custom was performed at numerous Holy Wells and the day was sometimes known as 'Shaking Bottle Sunday'. I have taken a drink myself, from this well, and had no following ill effects, but I would not recommend it for everyone.

The name of the village of Hinderwell was obviously derived from the name of the well, which shows that this Holy Well was there before people settled here and a legend has also survived the passage of time. It is said that St Hilda herself was once travelling up the coast with her retinue and because she was a little tired she rested by the roadside. Feeling rather thirsty she struck her staff into the ground and immediately there burst forth the sacred water that has never ceased flowing since that day. Similar legends have also been associated with various saints and their Holy Wells.

Another Holy Well named *Jacob's Well* is situated just over a mile to the west across country as the crow flies, from St Hilda's Well and lies just north of Barrowby along the narrow lane that leads eventually to Staithes. The well is set in a small triangle of common ground that lies between the lane and a cart track leading downhill to a farm. The water runs from beneath a stone retaining wall and is edged by a small curb before it disappears after a few yards under another larger stone.

The sound of running water can be heard beyond a nearby hedge but cannot be seen. This well is surrounded in spring and summer by a luxuriant growth of brambles and wild flowers and is hidden behind the branches of a diminutive tree that makes it difficult to find at those times of year. No special healing properties are known now, and the only claim it has to a sacred place is its name marked on an old map and the name of the surrounding area as being called Keld Hill derived from the Old English name 'Keld' meaning well.

Travelling north and west once more from Hinderwell and inland from Boulby Cliffs, the highest cliffs on the coast hereabouts, there is a Holy Well named *Three Crosses Well*. This is also marked on the Ordnance Survey map as an ancient monument and is set in a field beside a hawthorn hedge. All that remains is a half buried well-house with no signs of water but the reason for its title is supplied by three ancient cross bases lying on the ground beside it. There is little mention of this well in any known records but it is thought that, in the time of Cromwell when many village crosses were destroyed, someone decided to bring the remaining cross bases to this Sacred Spring for protection and in this way its original name, now forgotten, was so replaced.

Moving south from Hinderwell we come to the headland of

Kettleness and the site of Claymore Farm and here lies a famous Holy Well, named *Claymore Well,* from which the farm most probably took its name. This Holy Well is set deep in the ground beside the door of the farmhouse and, as in various other places, the land here was built up in a terrace in order to provide level ground on which to build. This meant that the well had to be surrounded by a retaining circle of stonework. Its only claim to fame is a legend which recounts that the fairies, the people of the hollow hills, were accustomed to washing their clothes here at this well and that the sound of their 'bittles' (a kind of wooden bat with which they beat the washing), could be heard as far away as Runswick Bay, more than a mile distant.

The famous abbey of Whitby, standing high on the headland overlooking the town, provides a wonderful landmark and St Hilda, who founded the abbey and to whom it is dedicated and lived there, surely knew where to build her church. Just below the abbey in a field known either by its correct name of Almshouse Close or the 'Donkey Field' as local people know it, there is a well named *Abbey Well* which is covered today by a curved arch of ancient brick (Figure 3). The land and the nearby great hall was owned in the early-1600s by Sir Hugh Cholmley who stated in his memoirs that:

> *The court levels which laid upon a hanging ground, unhandsomely,* [and] *very ill-watered, having only the Low Well, which is in the Almers-close, which I covered; and also discovered and erected the other adjoining conduit, and the wall in the courtyard, from whence I conveyed by leaden pipes, water into the house, brew-house, and wash-house.*

Figure 3. Abbey Well situated in Alms House Close just below Whitby Abbey.

This same 'Low Well' was assuredly the very same well which has been known locally for many years as *Abbey Well*. The water certainly rises as a spring from the ground and it never runs dry even in the longest drought when it still continues to issue forth from the well down the hillside and into the appropriately named Well Court below.

The most spectacular of all the Holy Wells in Yorkshire is the Sacred Spring of Newtondale which is set within the great gorge of that name lying a few miles inland from Whitby (Figure 4). The prolific spring water pours from a small aperture near the crest of the high cliff named Killing Nab Scar and falls as a sparkling cascade over large worked stones into a small shallow pool before descending

Figure 4. The spring and well at Newtondale.

down the hillside to the valley bottom. The water contains traces of iron and so the stones over which it runs are coloured a gloriously rich orange. The technical name for such impregnation is Chalybeate and this gives the water special tonic properties and is reputedly a cure for anaemia and associated diseases of the blood.

There is an old record of a man being cured of a disorder by bathing in the water of Newtondale in the year 1590. A man named Marshall writing in 1788 says of it, 'The waters have long been celebrated for their virtues in cold bathing and for the strengthening of limbs in children. This custom is still observed by neighbouring youths who come to this spring on certain days to bathe and to celebrate the virtues of the water.' In Goathland in 1885 a company was set up for the purpose of establishing a new health resort at Newtondale Spring, but this project did not come to fruition. It is known that a fair was once held here at midsummer when all the people of the neighbourhood would gather, 'in order to perform certain ceremonies which ensured them the blessing of the well', so says John Murray in his *Handbook for Travellers*, but he does not state what the ceremonies were.

Such a famous Holy Well is worth a visit if only for its spectacular

Figure 5. Hawsker, T'owd Abba Well. Of ancient origin, it is said that the waters from this well were pumped to Whitby Abbey

beauty. Whenever I go there I always drink of the water and bring away two bottles full to drink at home. A metal cup hanging from the railings surrounding a wooden platform over the water has been provided by the Forestry Commission who own the land and they have placed a wooden seat nearby. At my request also, they made a pathway through the trees and set up a signpost pointing the way to the well. It is a favourite place of mine.

If you take the A171 road from Whitby to Scarborough and then branch off onto the B1447 at Hawsker, you will find after a short while, on the left-hand side of the highway, a small, old brick building with a roof formed of just three great slabs of stone (Figure 5). A plaque once fixed to the end wall by Fylingdales Parish Council stated that this is *The Boiling Well.* Previous to this an older plaque on the wall proclaimed its more local name *'T'Awd Abba Well* (also known as the Old Boiling Well)'. So we find that this well, whilst being a definite Holy Well, has two names. On the Ordnance Survey map, the well is marked as T'Awd Abba Well.

The building is a fine example of a typical well-house associated with Holy Wells. The water of the spring is contained within a large tank inside. The wooden door is unfortunately set in the rear of the structure, which stands close to an old hawthorn hedge and this makes entry rather difficult. Inside, it can be found that at certain times the force of the spring rising up from the centre of the tank is so strong that the water appears to boil hence the name. The movement of the water of a Holy Well in this fashion, which happens on rare occasions, is said to have a healing property from the action, and it is from this action that the modern Jacuzzi was invented.

The older plaque also contained a rhyme that read as follows:

Lang centuries aback
This wor t'Awd Abba Well
Saint Hilda veiled i' black.
Lang centuries aback
Supped fra (from) it an' no lack
All t' sisterhood as well
Lang centuries aback
This wor t'Awd Abba Well.

This verse recalls that the land hereabouts, was once owned by Whitby Abbey, and it is believed that water from this well was piped to the abbey buildings for the use of the nuns.

Around fourteen miles to the west of Burniston, which is situated some distance from here on the main Scarborough-Whitby road, there stands a large area of conifer plantation called Cropton Forest. Through this a road leads northwards from Rawclife Top to Wheeldale Moor and beside this road and just five yards or so within the trees is the site of another ancient Holy Well named *Old Wife's Well*.

This well existed long before the trees were planted and is on the line of an old Roman road that once led over the moors from the Roman training camp at Cawthorne to a Roman signal station on the east coast. A signpost at the roadside points to the well that is also surrounded by a rustic fence in order to keep browsing deer away.

The water is held in a stone trough situated within a small simple stone construction fulfilling the definition of a well-house. Upright stones support a large lintel thus forming a mound that is covered over with turf. Along the lintel someone at some date has carved the name 'Nattie Fonten' but this work must have been carried out a very long time ago, as the letters are almost indecipherable. What the name means has been the subject of much argument over the years, but I have always wondered if the language used is not a form of ancient Norman or colloquial French.

No legend or healing properties attached to the well has survived, but the name of Old Wife refers to the old Pagan 'Earth Mother' and the well is sited along an old track known as 'Old Wife's Way'. This Holy Well has however attracted much attention lately as a Rag Well. Rag Wells were famed places where it was customary to carry out a certain form of healing that demanded a particular ritual. A shortened version of this procedure is that a piece of cloth torn from a garment worn by an ill person was taken to a Holy Well and tied to a nearby tree after being dipped in the water. As the rag deteriorated in the wind and weather so the illness of the patient would disappear.

On last visiting *Old Wive's Well* I found that the trees surrounding it were decorated with a large assortment of rags. There are still various Rag Wells even now being used in this fashion up and down the British Isles but there were once many more including quite a few within the Whitby area (Figure 6).

Not far from *Old Wive's Well* and still within Cropton Forest there is a Holy Well named *Roman Well*, a very attractive spring emerging straight from the ground and surrounded by a mass of Ladder Ferns. It is marked on old maps of the area and is set further upstream from a place where a bridge crosses the beck that runs through the valley lying north of the Roman camp at Cawthorne. Possibly the Roman soldiers were accustomed to drinking from this well as the name implies; the water is certainly crystal clear.

Figure 6. A typical example of a Rag Well as can be found throughout the world.

The village of Lastingham lies within a mile of the south-western boundary of Cropton Forest and it was here that St Cedd, the Saxon bishop founded a Christian monastery in AD 648. In this small village there are no less than three Holy Wells remaining, one being dedicated to the saint himself, and which is covered by a canopy of ornamental stonework (Figure 7). This is inscribed with a reference to St Cedd and, on the front of the well-house above a worn figure of a lion's

head, there is a tap from which at one time the weary traveller could obtain a refreshing drink. Sadly, today the authorities have decided that this spring water is not suitable for consumption and the tap is now connected to the general water main of the village. Ironically, the tap has to be turned off in the winter as the water freezes up, something spring water never does.

It is said that a long time ago, particular customs were

Figure 7. Lastingham, St Cedd's Well, under its ornate stone canopy. *Alan Whitworth*

performed here, but the local churchgoers of the period objected to this and the rites were discontinued. No one can state just what the customs consisted of but there was once a certain ritual performed at weddings hereabouts when the local lads raced for possession of the bride's garter - and presumably a kiss!

Another of the Holy Wells at Lastingham is sited round the corner from *St Cedd's Well* up the High Street. This well is named *St Chad's Well* after the brother of St Cedd and the one who took over the administration of the monastery after his brother died. The name St Chad is carved on the stone lintel of the well-house which is set into a retaining wall but the water from this well was piped away some time back. The reason for this it is said was because people came here to wash their motor cars and caused a certain amount of nuisance; others felt it was a desecration, and so used the above as an excuse to stop the practice.

A legend of this well tells how St Chad had a cell here. The son of the King of Mercia was hunting nearby and he caught site of a pure white hart and followed it through the trees until it came to the doorway of the monk's cell where it suddenly disappeared. Unable to understand this phenomenon he asked St Chad what had happened and the saintly man explained that the white hart had simply been a Christian symbol intended to lead the prince to his cell to be taught the new Christian religion. Being greatly impressed by the miracle the Prince agreed to be baptised and follow the Christian faith. Unfortunately, when the King, his father heard of his son's conversion he ordered the Prince to be killed for his abandonment of the old Pagan God's. Later however, the King repented of his action and he himself became a Christian.

The third Holy Well at Lastingham is set beside the main road that runs through the village. It is dedicated to St Ovin who, after his fall from grace as a high official at the court of Queen Ethelrid, came as a monk to the monastery here in order to serve out a penance. He later went with St Chad to Lichfield and ended his days at the monastery of Ely where a stone inscribed in Latin 'God Give to Ovin thy Light and Rest' covered his burial place. There is no water remaining at this well but what looks like one side of a trough is built into the back wall of the narrow well-house.

The name of 'Lady Well', or 'Well of Our Lady', is the most popular of all the names given to Holy Wells, and on the Castle headland at Scarborough there is a Sacred Well just so titled *Our Lady's Well*. The site of this well is near the cliff edge and just beside the boundary ditch of the former Roman Signal Station. Adjacent to the well are the remains of the medieval chapel of St Mary and an early Iron-Age settlement also once occupied this area. The reason for the strategic and sacred importance of this site over many centuries was obviously the presence of the water.

According to a modern guide-book the water of the well was held to be miraculous. This may have been so described because the water rose level with the ground whilst within the fortified keep of Scarborough Castle some hundred yards away it was necessary to dig down twenty feet in order to reach water. Nowadays the well is surrounded by a stone parapet, but because of modern drainage of the headland, the water is no longer in evidence.

Further down the Yorkshire coast at Reighton on the road from Filey to Bridlington, there exists a Holy Well named *St Helen's Well*, a name popularly given to many Holy Wells in the North of England. The well is situated on St Helen's Lane and has been lately restored but rather than a well-house, an ornamental pump has been placed over a large cistern containing the water. Also, at nearby Speeton, there is a Holy Well known as *Peggy Myer's Well* which is on a bank at the northern end of Wide Lane. Peggy Myers may have been a local character, but the name 'Peggy' is often a shortened version of St Margaret. Unfortunately, nothing more is known of these two wells beyond their identifying titles.

Closer to home, another Holy Well can be found in the village of Ugglebarnby, and is hidden away behind the parish church. To see it, take an old public footpath and bridleway leading behind the church which leads along the edge of a small valley. Set into the wall along the lower side of the footpath is an old gate. Pass through the gate

and down the flight of steps that lead to a small stone well-house. The beautiful clear water inside runs into a stone trough and I have been told that the local people used it not so very long ago as their source of drinking water. The stone ledge of the trough shows signs of wear by buckets as people took the water away. I know of no legends or folk tales associated with this well, but on old maps it is titled *Foss Hill Well* and so because of being named it has a claim to being a genuine Holy Well.

Of the other type of wells, the artesian variety, a number of these are named and may have their origins as Holy Wells. One

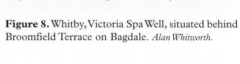

Figure 8. Whitby, Victoria Spa Well, situated behind Broomfield Terrace on Bagdale. *Alan Whitworth.*

Figure 9. Whitby, Victoria Spa Well house in 1844, from an engraving by the local artist George Weatherill.

in particular is that in Whitby, where, behind Broomfield Terrace on the downward road of Bagdale into the town, a small Victorian edifice covers a water source (Figure 8). This is an ever-flowing natural spring that emerges from the ground of its own accord. The water of the spring, which once poured into a stone trough, contains within it a certain amount of iron mineral salts and from time immemorial the local people drank the water as it was looked on as having health-giving properties.

This spring has all the attributes of a Holy Well and must have existed for a very long time. Indeed, a drawing by the Whitby artist George Weatherill dated 1844, shows a building standing on its own in Bagdale and set amidst a glade of shrubs and trees (Figure 9). This later fell into disrepair and became lost.

Around the year 1860 a man named John Stevenson bought land in Bagdale in order to erect there a terrace of houses. It seems that he was unaware of the fact that the spring or ancient Holy Well, with its stone trough, stood within the area that he intended to develop. It

Figure 10. Interior of the Victoria Spa Well house, Whitby, showing the ornate pump and decorative woodwork. *Alan Whitworth.*

was while workmen were digging out the foundations that the stone trough was rediscovered.

As Stevenson could not divert the water, nor could he build houses over it, he decided to give the well its own small circular well-house with a conical lantern roof with coloured glass skylights. Inside he set a pump wherewith to draw the water from below, and also provided a white marble hand basin and a little semicircular wooden seat (Figure 10). A door gave access so that people could sit and drink the health-giving water. This building was given the name Victoria Spa to fall in with the fashion of the day.

A report in the *Whitby Times* of 28 September 1888, states that, 'The Victoria Spa in Bagdale, near the burial ground of the Friends, is chalybeate and belongs to Mr John Stevenson, chemist.'

'The analysis of the water by H. Medlock, Esquire, of London, gives the following constituents in an imperial gallon :-

Chloride of Sodium	4,2966 grains
Chloride of Potassium	5,3006 grains
Carbonate of Potassium	4373 grains
Sulphate of Lime	4,6323 grains
Carbonate of Lime	7,0624 grains
Carbonate of Magnesia	3,4557 grains
Carbonate of Protoxide of Iron	2,2769 grains
Silica	3080 grains
Organic Matter	1,4630 grains
Carbonate of Magnesia	traces

'After giving an analytical table of the Tunbridge Wells waters by way of comparison, Mr Medlock remarked that the Whitby water in question closely resembles the Tunbridge Wells chalybeate but the quantity of iron is smaller. 'I should be disposed,' he adds, 'to consider the Whitby water very near equal in medicinal properties to that of Tunbridge Wells. As the iron exists in the most active form of pro-carbonate, the water will doubtless prove a valuable tonic.'

'The water flows into a stone receptacle within a rustic alcove. Tickets for the Season are furnished by Mr Stevenson. We have been informed that these waters were at one time free to the public.'

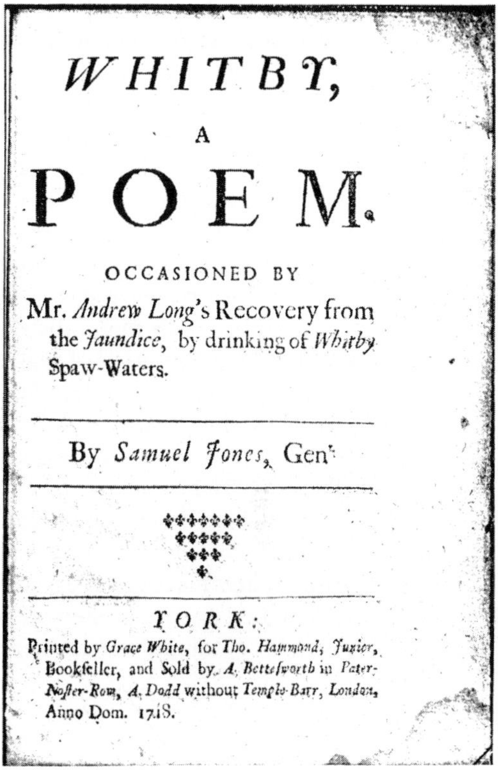

WHITBY,
A
POEM.
OCCASIONED BY
Mr. *Andrew Long*'s Recovery from the *Jaundice*, by drinking of *Whitby* Spaw-Waters.

By *Samuel Jones*, Gen^t.

YORK:
Printed by *Grace White*, for *Tho. Hammond*, *Junior*, Bookseller, and Sold by *A. Bettesworth* in *Pater-Noster-Row*, *A. Dodd* without *Temple-Barr*, *London*, Anno Dom. 1718.

Figure 11. In the eighteenth century, Spa waters at Whitby were regularly drunk, and were so famous they inspired a poem about their healing properties.

In 1910 there was a small cottage beside the Quaker Burial Ground across the way from the spa, which was called *Park Cottage* and which was owned by a Mr Bonus. It was his daughter Annie who took care of the 'Spa' and held the key to the door. It was she who drew the waters and dispensed it to the public at two pence a glass per day or two shillings and sixpence (half a crown) for a monthly supply.[1]

In 1918 the Mineral Water Factory at the rear of Broomfield Terrace owned by John Stevenson and associated with Stevenson's spa, was sold to Charles Tindale, however, the Victoria Spa Well did not form part of the sale.

Fortunately, the beautiful little well-house still remains. There is still a semi-circular wooden seat inside and the interior all covered in white tiles, is still lit by a roof lantern with coloured glass panes. And although the white basin survives with its brass pump shaped like a swan and set into the wall, the pipe from the pump is no longer connected to the spring water that still flows beneath the floor of the small building. It appears that some time ago the beck, known as

Bagdale Beck which was once open and navigable beyond this point but that now runs below the road in Bagdale became contaminated with blood from a slaughter-house nearby. This subsequently overflowed into the spring water and so made it unfit to drink.

Scarborough Borough Council, who are responsible for this Grade II listed Victorian Spa have been approached recently with a request to restore the supply of water once more, as the slaughter-house no longer stands and the waters of Bagdale Beck do not appear to flood into the spring - but it is doubtful that the water will ever be sold again for two pence a glass!

Two other wells in the district are worthy of mention. The first can be found in the parish of Ugglebarnby, standing beside the highway at Hempsyke, a small hamlet in that parish. Within the sandstone rubble wall is set a trough in a square-headed niche. Above the trough the water flows from the mouth of a marble lion's head (Figure 12). The well was restored by John Hempsyke in the year 1856, but the lion's head is earlier in date, and undoubtedly the well is much earlier still. The wall above is shaped to encompass a semicircular inset panel carved with the name 'A HEMPSYKE'.

Attached to the stonework within the niche are three engraved plaques containing verses that read as follows:

Weary stranger here you see
An emblem of true Charity.
Richly my bounty I bestow
Made by a kindly hand to flow
And I have fresh supplies from Heaven
For every cup of water given.
John Allen Hempsyke 1856.

This stream is pure as if from
Heaven it ran
And while praise the Lord
I'll thank the man.
Tramp 1861.

Man made the trough
The water God bestows
Then praise his name
From whom the blessing flows.
John Allen Hempsyke 1856

Today this remarkable monument is protected as a structure of architectural and historic interest, and listed Grade II by English Heritage.

The second well, also in the parish of Ugglebarnby, is that at Falling Foss, east of *Newton House*. Falling Foss is a well-known waterfall in the district near the hamlet of Littlebeck, whose waters drop down an escarpment sixty-seven feet in height.[2] Here on the estate of *Newton House* stands a well-head and obelisk said to date from around 1882 and erected to commemorate the transformation of the moorland into a pleasure garden. While the obelisk itself may only be of nineteenth century date, the foundations of *Newton House* are quite old, and near to the waterfall of Falling Foss there is a hermitage hewn out of a solid piece of stone, so it is quite probable that the water of the well here may too be of ancient origin.

The handsome obelisk is built of tooled sandstone and ashlar masonry and has a wooden sluice gate. It is square on plan and stands on a stepped plinth below a tall die with an overhanging flat cap on which is placed the obelisk itself. The east and west sides of the die carry Latin inscriptions. The east side inscription reads:

Quae dat aquas, saxo laiet
Hospita nympha sub imo
Sic tu cum dederis dona,
Latere relis
Nesciat sinsitra Quid
Dextra porrigat.[3]

The west side inscription is largely illegible, but the name Ionas Browne (John Browne) and the characters '—LXXXII' are still visible.

Today, we take our water supplies for granted. No longer do we venerate our wells, whether 'holy' or otherwise. Many have disappeared, and often, only the place-name 'Holy Well' survives to indicate the probable existence of just such a well as in the case of 'Holy Well' at Liverton Mines, and at Fylingthorpe, where the

Figure 12. Ugglebarnby, John Hempsyke's Well. Here we see the eighteenth century lion's head from possibly an earlier well house on the site.

Fylingdales Inn was once a house named 'Holywell' and bears the date 1907. Others where they do survive are now dry through neglect, poor maintenance or the deliberate diversion of the water. At Hawsker, beside the road leading out toward Robin Hood's Bay a well there bears the inscription and date 'TC 1790' and is just such an example.

With climatic changes in the air perhaps this is the time to reconsider the importance of our wells as nothing can be taken for granted – no one knows just what is round the corner, which makes one wonder if possibly they should be treated with more consideration and respect?

Notes and References

1. This piece of information was provided by Mr Harold Brown, the historian from Whitby Museum. He was the nephew of Mr Bonus, and who remembers visiting his uncle in his cottage, which now no longer exists.

2. Horne's *Guide to Whitby*. Ninth edition, 1904.

3. ibid.; The translation of this rhyme kindly supplied by the Rev. Barry Williams reads:

> *Kindly nymph, the water's given,*
> *Grant beneath these rocks the river,*
> *May forever flow,*
> *what your right hand may provide,*
> *Pouring waters from your side,*
> *May your left hand never know.*

4. THE CLOUGHTON WHALES

by Ben Chapman

THERE CAN BE FEWER SIGHTS that stir the emotions than that of a stranded whale. To see one of these majestic leviathans of the deep stretched out lifeless on some inhospitable beach is truly heart-rending. This country is not only surrounded by water, but by beaches of every description, many of which have become the fatal resting place for all types of cetaceans.

Not far from the popular seaside town of Scarborough on the Yorkshire coast is an insignificant place called Cloughton Wyke, where two whale strandings took place in the year 1910. The first occurred on 27 March, and involved a female common Rorqual Whale measuring fifty-one feet in length. The *Scarborough Mercury* dated 1 April 1910, printed under the heading, 'The Stranded Whale';

PROBLEM OF ITS DISPOSAL

What to do with the stranded whale at Cloughton Wyke is a puzzle confronting the authorities. The last whale stranded in this neighbourhood cost about £30 to remove, and it is estimated that this will cost about £50. Tenders will be issued for its removal, but no one seems anxious to have the job, and the Board of Trade, who are responsible for its removal naturally want the cost to be as little as possible. The difficulties in regard to removing the present whale are each day that passes will make its removal more unpleasant, it weighs about fifty tons, and is situated in an inaccessible part, just at the foot of the cliff. It will have to be cut up, conveyed to the sands in a boat, and then carted away and buried.

The second whale, and the subject of this article was also a female common Rorqual, but slightly larger measuring seventy-two feet in length, which was washed ashore on 12 September in the same year (Figures 1 and 2).

The common Rorqual, or Fin Whale, is one of the five main Rorquals, so named because of their plicated throats, after the Norwegian word for 'furrow'. These concertina-like pleats are simply a means of stretching the whale's throat when gathering food. The small organisms the whale consumes are collectively called Krill, this

Whale washed ashore near Scarborough Sep. 12.

Figures 1 and 2 Photographs of the whale beached at Cloughton on 12 September 1910.

MONSTER WHALE STRANDED AT CLOUGHTON WYKE

Figures 3 and 4 Raising up the carcass of the whale at Cloughton on 15 September 1910.

Krill is drawn into the mouth amid gallons of water, which in turn is forced back out again through gill strainers of balleen, formerly known as whalebone and widely used in the manufacture of ladies stays and corsets. The Krill is then forced down the whale's throat with the tongue and the feeding process is repeated.

The *Scarborough Mercury* again reported this stranding on 16 September 1910.

ANOTHER LEVIATHAN STRANDED

Whales must have a partiality for Cloughton. Another one has been washed up there, and for the second time within a few months the authorities will have to face the question of removing a huge carcass that could soon become a danger to public health. The last leviathan was removed by a Scarborough man, after it had diffused an offensive odour in the district and attracted thousands to the scene of the stranding. There will be another reason for coast pilgrimages, and no doubt paragraph writers and photographers will not neglect the opportunity. The whale is said to be larger than the first one. It is stranded half a mile further north than the one that washed ashore at Easter, the exact place being Sychram Point. It is 72 feet in length, whilst the girth is fifty feet, the weight is variously estimated up to eighty tons. It is stated that the odour given out by the whale is even more offensive that that emitted by the previous one, and can be detected before the whale is sited. There are no marks suggestive of the whale being harpooned, and it appears that it has been carried to Cloughton by a strong inward current. On Monday the leviathan was lying well down on the beach, but the night tide moved it, and it is now lying higher up. The coastguards are taking steps to have the carcass removed as it is already a danger to health. The whale will no doubt be cut up and buried in lime as was the last one, and the cost may be anything up to fifty pounds. The whale was reported by a Captain of a Spanish steamer which arrived in the Tyne, as having been seen five miles off Whitby, where it was in direct line of the coasting vessels and a danger to shipping. On Tuesday, postcard views of the whale were on sale in Scarborough and many people have seen the whale itself since its stranding.

In the event, the carcass was not towed away but cut up on the beach, winched up the cliff face, and carted away by a horse slaughterer named Mark Bennett aided by some local men (Figures 3 and 4). It was said at the time that Mr Bennett had the whale jaw bones set up as an archway leading to his farmhouse on the Burniston coast road.

5. The Rise and Fall of East Coast Fishing

by Alma Brunton

The fishermen brave more money have
Than any merchants two or three;
Therefore I will to Scarborough go,
That I a fisherman brave may be.[1]

FISHING HAS ALWAYS BEEN BIG BUSINESS since the end of the Middle Ages, and disputes in the industry have involved kings, government and even the various Churches at differing periods. The history of the British fishing industry is a story of violence, suffering and death; a constant struggle with the sea, the elements and human enemies(Figure 1). Wars have been waged over the right to fish in various areas of the seas, and fishermen have been executed for fishing in someone else's territory. Thankfully, dangers of this kind have largely disappeared, but the battle with nature is not yet won, nor will it ever be. In 1974 one of our very best and most modern trawlers, the *Gaul*, disappeared with her crew of thirty-six men, and it is only in very recent years has the sea yielded her up. And recently

Figure.1 Herring cobles in the ninetenth century running to a harbour in a gale.

Figure 2. Whitby harbour in the 1950s, where fishermen mending their nets could be watched by the many tourists who flocked here.

in the first month of the twenty-first century a modern fishing boat *Solway Harvester* made the news headlines by her disappearance under mysterious circumstances with the loss of her entire crew.

The sailors who man today's fishing craft are, perhaps for the first time ever, adequately paid for their labours, and many a shore-worker envies the fisherman his pay packet (Figure 2). The fish in the sea belong to no one; there is nothing to stop anyone from buying a boat, and becoming a fisherman – if he can, and dares! With changes in the industry and fishing quotas often in the news lately this brief article is an attempt to put the rise and fall of the fishing industry into perspective.

No one can be certain just how or when fishing in the North Sea began, but there is evidence to show that it dates back to Roman times, for fishing craft from that period have been found in river estuaries. The Vikings, who invaded Yorkshire's coast in the ninth century, were known to be fishermen – in fact, it has been suggested that herring fishing may have been one reason for their interest hereabouts. There was a migration of herring to England's eastern shores at this date, and Vikings may have been following the shoals when they sited our shores. As early as 836AD the Netherlanders are said to have visited the North-East coast of Britain for the purpose of buying 'Saltfish', and herring almost certainly comprised part of this trade (Figure 3).

Figure.3 Herring coble going to sea.

Figure 4. A group of fishermen at Scarborough in a traditional coble, a design said to be based on the Viking longship.

Figure 5. The Scotch herring fleet at Whitby.

Another indication of just how seriously fishing was taken is given by the fact that boats from the East Coast were regularly visiting Iceland by the twelfth century. This was a staggering enterprise when one considers that the boats they used were really nothing more than large open rowing boats, with a mast and single sail (Figure 4). Interestingly, even in those far off days, the Icelanders complained that the English were ruining their fishing!

Around 1536 John Leland (c.1506-52), the first Englishman to write a description of almost the whole of the country from personal observation, wrote of Whitby, that it was a 'great fisher town'.[2] Indeed, at that date, fishing was the only significant industry with little competition and no scarcity of prey.

Controlled by the monastery of St Hilda, perched high on the cliff-tops above the small haven, when the new monastery was founded about the year 1100 and William de Percy was Abbot, there arose a difference between him and the Prior of Bridlington concerning the tithes relating to fish. The account given of the dispute, favours the view that there was already a settled trade and that the fishermen did not confine themselves to their own immediate coast. The men of Filey sometimes landed at Whitby – the men of Whitby at Filey; the matter of contention was consequently as to the place where the tithe should be paid. In settlement it was ordered that payment should be made where the fish was landed to the monastery in which port it was landed.[3] This arrangement continued for nearly one hundred years until about 1191, when, because of the discontent of the brotherhood at Bridlington, the Abbot of Rievaulx, the Prior of Kirkham and the Prior of Warter, acting as the Pope's commissioners in a further dispute on the matter, decided that the monks of Whitby should not take tithe from the fishermen of Filey landing there.[4]

In the year 1248 litigation began as to the rights of the respective parties, but an amicable agreement was arrived at, one of the terms of settlement being that the Abbot and convent of Whitby should deliver yearly, to such person as the Master and Brotherhood should appoint, 'three thousand good and seasonable herrings on the morrow of St Andrew the Apostle, at Thornton le Dale in the Vale of Pickering, for ever.'[5] 'As for the three thousand herrings,' says Charlton, the Whitby historian writing in 1779, 'they still continue payable to the Archbishop of York, on the before-mentioned day of the year, not at Thornton but at his Palace at Bishopthorpe.'[6] It was the same when Young wrote in 1817; moreover he tells us, agreeing with what Charlton wrote, the Archbishop 'receives yearly as composition for the tithe of fish taken at Whitby and Robin Hood's Bay one hundred good stock fish, or 26s 8d in money; two hundred dried cod and ling of the best sort, delivered at Michaelmas, and four loads of fresh fish of the best and largest packing, viz. two loads in each of the assize weeks.'[7]

There are surviving several Customs accounts (in Latin) giving interesting particulars relating to fish traffic at the port of Whitby as far back as the thirteenth and fourteenth century. The duties imposed by King Edward I on the goods of 'aliens' (foreign merchants) and which became known as 'the new Custom', also sometimes as 'Aliens Custom' and at other times 'Petty Custom',[8] gave occasion for some of the accounts. Threepence in the pound on the price was the duty payable by foreign merchants on herrings brought in (Figure 5).

One of these accounts,[9] rendered by Robert de Barton and Gilbert de Bedeford, appears to furnish exact figures concerning herrings liable to the new Custom brought into Whitby 'from the fourth day of July in the 32nd year of the reign of Lord Edward, illustrious King of England [1304], until the Feast of Saint Michael next following.' The total value of dutiable herrings accounted for as having been brought in during the stated period was £40 13s 4d, the new Custom amounting to 10s 2d.

Further examples of entries in the account under notice include on the 23 July, 'the ship of Farbold del Ways' which brought in half a last of herrings,[10] priced 26s 8d. On the twenty-sixth of the same month, 'the ship of John, son of William del Estend,' brought in three lasts valued at 100 shillings. This is the largest cargo accounted and the highest valued. 'The ship of John Loth' on 6 August, brought in 1000 herrings, priced 6s 8d. On 11 August 'the ship of Walter Athelard' brought in three lasts, priced £4 6s 8d.; and on the 20

September, 'the ship of Lambert del Wayn' brought in 2000 herrings, priced 10s, and 'the ship of Walter Ditland' two lasts priced four pounds.

A similar Customs account relating to Whitby is available with respect to part of the following reign of King Edward II (1307-27), the account being that of Henry of Boston and Adam of Pykering, the collectors of the new Custom, and extending from, 8 June 1315 until, 12 April 1317. This account specifies the price or value but not the quantity of each load of herrings. Ten shillings is the smallest value entered in the account and fifty shillings the highest, duty on the latter amount having been found to be payable on the 20 August by 'John, son of Hugh of Huflet.' The total value of herrings entered as liable to the duty during the period over which the account dates was £40, the new Custom on this value being ten shillings.[11]

In the year 1394 prodigious shoals of herrings appeared off the port of Whitby which occasioned a vast influx of foreign fishermen who bought up and cured the fish and exported it, to the great injury of the natives. To prevent this the King issued a proclamation directed to the bailiffs of 'liberty of the church of Saint Hilda of Whitby' requiring them to put a stop to the practice.[12]

The monks would not lack fish for their fast days, or for their feast days, and after supplying their own wants they were able to sell the surplus. Between 11 November 1394 and, 30 May 1395, they received for fish sold £42 8s 3d.[13] In 1396 their receipts for tithe and net money for the half year from Whitsuntide to Martinmas were £52 13s 6d or thereabouts. They account for the sale of coal fish and codlings; of good herrings at four pounds, and of worse at two pounds the last, while three thousand white herrings in the fish-house were reckoned to be worth 21s 6d.[14]

There is extant a roll of the time of Henry IV (1399-1413) relating to the collection at 'Whythby and Hertylpole' (Whitby and Hartlepool) of the subsidy known as 'poundage' – an impost levied on the value of most goods imported or exported. The rate of this impost varied in amount during the reign of King Henry IV, but for the period to which the account under notice applies 1404 and 1413, the rate was twelvepence in the pound. The Whitby section, in Latin, extends from the 16 June to 20 October. The exports included in the account consisted wholly of herrings, variously specified as salted herrings, white herrings salted and white herrings in barrel. The value of the herrings stated in the account to have been exported was – in the month of July £96; in August £66 10s; in September £25; and in the included portion of October £53 10s – the prices varying from two pound to £4 13s 4d per last.

To promote the fishing industry, and, indirectly, the interests of the Navy, by increasing the consumption of fish, it was directed in an Act relating to the Navy passed in the year 1652, that with the exception of the Wednesdays in Christmas and Easter weeks every Wednesday throughout the year which was not already a 'fish-day' should be observed as such, and the Act forbade, on pain of fine or imprisonment, any person to eat flesh on any then existing 'fish-day', or on any Wednesday newly required to be observed as such. Thirteen years later there seems to have been some fear that the eating of flesh on Wednesdays would be again allowed, and the Public Record Office, contains a representation, dated 10 March 1575,[15] which reads literally:

> *Wee whose names bee hereunto subscribed doo testifie and wilbe redy to prove that the Townes and places whiche are heare underneath written are encreased of sea fisher botts and barks from ten ton of burden to xxx tons to the number of cxl sayles from the tyme of the makinge of the statute from abstynence of fleshe on the Wednesday until this presente – And if the said lawe had not bin made, wherby those botts and barks are increased so many in nomber, or rather more, wolde have bin decayed within this realme: And therefore wee are of the opynyon if the said lawe shulde no longer induer that it wolde be in manner an utter decaying of all the whole fishermen within this realme, and so when soever the Quene's matie, shulde have any occacion to send her Highness' ships to the Seas there wolde not be founde sea faringe men to man the same.*

The names of sundry fishing towns, including Whitby, are appended and followed by twenty-two signatures.

A considerable fishing trade was not without some disadvantage, however. An order dated July 1636, was made by the North Riding Quarter Sessions for the setting up of a House of Correction at Whitby for the parishes of Whitby, 'Lyeth', Sneaton, and Hinderwell, the reason given :

> *that the trade of fishing doth in those partes increase a multydute of poore who, in winter tyme, when the said trade*

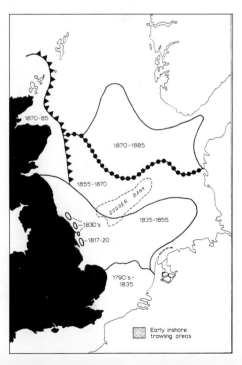

Figure 6. Map showing the spread of trawling across the North Sea, based on a similar in Yorkshire Coast Fishing Industry 1780-1914.

faileth, are either driven to begg or wander, or else cast upon the chardges of severall parishes, which, without some mean of correcting and setting them to worke, are noe way able to relieve soe greate a multydute of poore and idle persons drawne thither from diversem places, who being of stronge and bale bodyes doe not onely refuse to labour but comitt diverse outragess and misdemeanours.

Sir Hugh Cholmley and Sir John Hotham, to whose charge the matter was remitted, found a house at the Flowergate end of Cliff Lane that answered the purpose.[16] This building is still in existence today.

In spite of its importance during the Middle Ages, the herring fishery was later to be rivalled by that for white fish. Before the early fifteenth century, Scarborough and Whitby vessels were exploiting the cod grounds off the Faroe Islands and Iceland and such activities continued into the seventeenth century.[17] However, the middle of that century appears to have been a watershed for the Yorkshire coast fishing industry. The upheavals associated with the Civil War and the loss of many larger craft to the Dutch seem to have ended the northern voyages from Scarborough and Whitby.[18] Interest in herring fishing also seems to have declined markedly, so that by the following century it was of little more than local importance where previously it had been a national industry. Yet among this decline there is evidence of growth. Yorkshire craft travelled in considerable numbers to Yarmouth each year to participate in its still prosperous autumn herring fishery. At other times of the year more attention was given to the white fish grounds in the North Sea, especially of the Dogger Bank where larger cod were being taken (Figure 6).

Three types of fishing techniques have been employed at different periods. Firstly, was the line method, where a great length of fishing line about three miles long with numerous hooks at six feet intervals was trailed from a boat (Figure 7). Each hook was individually baited with mussels, which had to be opened and attached by hand. This

Figure 7. Line fishing from a coble. Although only small the line would extend out over a mile and take in perhaps a ton of fish.

task, known as scaning, was often undertaken by a fisherman's wife or his children (Figure 8). Then the whole line was carefully wound into coils on a cairn or skep until the pile was quite high. The sight of young wives carrying these bundles of lines was a common one in the small ports and harbours on the North-East coast. This fishing technique was and still is suitable for small-scale enterprises employed by small fishing craft.

In later years, as the demand for fish became greater, and the prey scarcer, drifting began to be seen in coastal waters (Figure 9). Here, a deep net was suspended from floats and hung down, held between two boats. As the day's fishing came to an end these two craft would draw the net to a close in an encircling movement, trapping the fish in the circle of the net and eventually as the net was hauled aboard the fish would be dragged up with it.

Lastly, came trawling where a large close-ended net is dragged along the sea bottom for miles, its mouth held open by huge metal 'otter' boards which also help to weight it down. When this method of fishing was first introduced in the nineteenth century it was both hated and feared by the traditional fishermen. Here

Figure 8. Mary Mansfield, 1870, a 'flither girl'. Such women as these went out and collected the mussels used for line bait.

was an indiscriminate method of catching fish where many where killed or tossed back into the sea badly damaged to die later. Young, old, sick of whatever variety scooped up, as a consequence it was said that fish stocks were in danger of becoming depleted, and perhaps with the scarcity of fish today, those fears were not unfounded!

Mary Linskill wrote *In and About Whitby* in 1888 which was

Figure 9. Lowestoft herring Drifters out at sea. From the 1930s to the late 1950s herring boats from the south and from Scotland were a common sight in Northern harbours, especially Scarborough and Whitby, wherever, the annual 'Whitby Regatta' was staged around the Scotch Herring fleet's traditional visit (see also Figure 5).

serialised in the *Whitby Gazette* that year. In this analysis of Whitby town and its environs, she relates the words of an old fisherman on the subject of trawling.

Opinion seems to vary greatly in the scientific world as to the damage really done by trawling, but there is only one opinion on this point among the fisher-folk of Whitby and neighbourhood – it is that trawling has raised the place as a fishing ground.

"Ah've been a fisherman iver se Ah was a bairn," said a picturesque old man with a sou'wester newly-painted with yellow ochre, and a blue guernsey much toned down with the salt water. His rugged face was full of character, lined and bronzed, and weather-beaten. *"Ah went wi' boats when Ah wa that high,"* he replied in answer to my question as to his acquaintance with the fisheries of Whitby. *"An I' them daays, an' for lang aneaff [enough] afther, one boat wad fetch in as much five as five-an-twenty'll fetch noo [now]."*

"And what do you consider to be the cause of the falling off?"

"The cause of it" (with emphatic manner of speech, and tragic gesture), *"The cause on it? Why trawlin', to be sure, nowt else! The fish isn't there! It's killed wi' the trawlers. An' they doan't only kill the fish I' the sea; they detsroy the spawn at the bottom on it. There's hundreds o' tons o' spawn, an' dead fish thrawn back into the watter... Did ya iver see a trawl?"*

"No: I have seen a drawing of one."

"Then mebbe ya could see for yerself, an' understand hoo [how] a mass o' wood an' iron like that dragged ower the groond where the spawn lies 'll destroy all it comes near!"

"And you think that the present scarcity of fish on this coast is entirely owing to that? You know of no other reason?"

"There isn't no other reason! The fish was there, year by year till the trawlers came. Why Ah've seen as many as fifty score o' great fine cod

Figure 10. Traditional cobles in Whitby harbour in the nineteenth century.

*an' ling laid to dry at once upon this vary bit o' pier end where we're
stannin."*

"And how many are laid now, in the height of season?"

"None! None!" almost shouted the old man. 'The plaace is rewinded
[ruined]; - *as Ah said afore, it's rewined!"*

In earlier times a wide range of fishing vessels was to be found,[19] but
from the seventeenth century onwards designs were based on
variants of the age-old cobble derived from the boats of the Vikings
(Figure 10). The largest of these variants were known as 'five-man
boats'. They were already in use at Whitby before the dissolution of
the monasteries to take coal to the Abbey,[20] and they are referred to
in Scarborough fishermen's wills from at least the later sixteenth
century. Sometime between 1650 and 1750 however, they evolved
into single-keeled, three-masted, decked 'luggers' which were to
form the mainstay of the Yorkshire coast off-shore fleet well into the
nineteenth century (Figure 11).

Throughout those centuries and beyond, fisherfolk had to contend
with the violence of the sea and occasionally other men in their hunt
for a livelihood. Their unique and often over-romanticised
occupation has thus set them apart (Figure 12). Nevertheless danger
was ever present and death an all too constant companion. The
insularity of the fishing communities and the vicissitudes and

Figure 11. A mixture of cobles and 'three-men' masted-boats beside the Fish Pier,
Scarborough.

uncertainty that were part and parcel of their way of life was strongly reflected in their customs, superstitions and folklore. Naturally, these differed from neighbouring agricultural villages but even in an age when English folk tradition remained vigorous, fishing communities were considered to be strongly tinctured with superstition. Luck in particular was a commodity to be nurtured. In order, no doubt, to encourage good fortune the fishermen of sixteenth century Redcar invited their friends to a festival held upon St Peter's Day 'with a free hearte and no show of niggardness.' Their boats were decorated, masts painted and during the course of the celebrations each craft was sprinkled with good liquor sold to the fishermen at a groat a quart.[21] Even today, the annual ceremony of 'Blessing the Boats' is held at Whitby, when the Bishop of Whitby holds a service on the harbour wall and sprinkles holy water on the ships tied up alongside. At Flamborough it was considered that a good season's fishing would follow the custom of 'Raising Herrings'. When the men had left for the fishery, their wives and other folk disguised themselves, often in garments of their male relations, and went round the village with music and laughter, visiting their neighbour's houses to receive alms and 'God Speed'.[22] Filey also maintained a tradition believed to encourage herrings. On the third Saturday night after the boats had sailed for Yarmouth fishery, youngsters would seize all the unused

Figure 12. Fisher girls packing herring on the Fish Pier, at Scarborough.

wagons and carts then drag them to the cliff top, leaving them to be taken away by their owners on the Sunday morning; this ritual was believed to drive the herrings into the nets. Bad omens often deterred fishermen from sailing. If a Flamborough fisherman met a woman, parson or a hare on his way to the boats he would turn back immediately in the belief that he would have no luck that day.[23] This was also true of Whitby fishermen. At Staithes it was also considered ill-luck for a fisherman to meet a woman while he walked down to the boats carrying lines on his head or nets on his shoulder. When a woman saw a fisherman approaching under such circumstances she would at once turn her back on him. All four-footed animals were also considered to be unlucky with the mention of the pig's name being the unluckiest. Similarly, an egg was deemed such an ill-omen that Staithes fishermen would not call it such, but referred to it as a 'roundabout'.

Interestingly, as the influence of Methodism grew in the nineteenth century, many fishing families became noted for their piety, but some customs of pre-Christian origin remained. As

Figure 13. A modern trawler alongside Whitby dock.

late as the 1880s, one custom said to be secretly maintained at Staithes, had ancient origins. When a fishing boat had a protracted run of bad luck the wives of the owners and crew would assemble at midnight. Then, in deep silence, they would slay a pigeon whose heart was extracted, stuck full of pins and burnt over a charcoal fire. A witch was deemed the source of the bad luck although he or she was unconscious of their power of evil. While this ceremony was in progress the witch was supposed to come to the door, dragged there unwillingly by the irresistible potency of the charms and the conspirators would make the individual some propitiatory present. It was also said to be a frequent occurrence for Staithes fishermen to keep the first fish that came into a boat after many nights of catching nothing and on returning home burn it as a sacrifice to the fates.[24]

In Whitby, as the ship building trade increased, its fishing industry diminished. When Young was writing his history in the early years of the nineteenth century, there were said to be only nine fishermen, whilst in 1816 the number of seamen totalled 2,674.[25] Thenceforward, the principal fishery enterprise for a period was carried on from the neighbouring coast villages of Robin Hood's Bay, Staithes and Runswick. Around the year 1906 the number of fishermen in Whitby was 150 or thereabouts; and it was said that they did not adventure far, their only craft being the useful coble with her crew of three hands.[26]

By the early twentieth century all sectors of the Yorkshire coast fishing industry were in decline. The labour force reached its zenith in 1881 when a total of 1,632 fishermen were counted; by the year 1911 the total number had dropped slightly to 1,181 and a number of these were part-timers.[27] Stations such as Staithes and Filey, which had once sustained significant and sizeable fishing fleets in their own right, had been reduced to the status of inshore bases and the brief resurgence of Bridlington Quay and Whitby as off-shore fishing centres was still decades away. In part, such a falling away was to be expected as the trawling sector of the trade became increasingly sophisticated and centred on ports with considerable harbour facilities and marine engineering back-up (Figure 13). Yet, in part, decline was also a consequence of the pace of earlier expansion and growth and the lack of adequate conservation measures which led to a denudation of many North Sea white fishing grounds and a rush to open up new deep water fisheries in the far north. The resultant reliance upon such grounds off the coasts of other nations was to be at the root of many problems afflicting the British fishing industry during the latter part of the twentieth century; and the 'Cod War' with Iceland and troubles between English and Spanish fishing fleets, led eventually to its demise at the dawn of the new millennium.

★   ★   ★   ★   ★

When Britain entered World War Two, the Germans knew that if they were to succeed they must first destroy Britain's dominance on the sea. Accordingly, they launched a massive mine-laying exercise in an attempt to make all England's seaways impassable – this would not only damage our own shipping, but would also have the effect of dissuading neutral vessels from bringing much needed supply boats into our waters. During the course of the war the German navy laid more than forty thousand mines, of which a large proportion where situated in the North Sea.

Fortunately for England, Admiral Lord Charles Beresford had foreseen the possibility of this occurrence, and after a visit to East

Figure 14. The damage to the steam trawler *Passing* seen here in Scarborough harbour, after striking a mine in December 1914.

Coast ports in 1907 he recommended the use of steam trawlers as mine sweepers in the event of war. In answer to argument, Admiral Beresford pointed out the simple logic that in wartime, trawlers would not be able to fish anyway, and using them as mine sweepers would free naval vessels for other duties. On top of this, fishermen were undoubtedly the best men for the dangerous job of mine sweeping, for they were used to handling wires and trawls and they knew the coastline of the North Sea better than most. As a result of the decision that was taken to accept Admiral Beresford's recommendation, the rank of 'Skipper RNR' was to appear in navy lists for the first time.

At eight o'clock on a beautiful clear morning the trawlers set about their deadly work off Cayton Bay, steaming with sweeps streaming out to cut the wires that anchored the mines to the seabed. Within five minutes of beginning operations, eighteen mines had been exploded, and the senior officer realised that this was perhaps the densest minefield he had ever encountered. As the work progressed the tide fell rapidly, which in turn brought the mines nearer the surface and closer to the keels of the boats. Before long the inevitable happened and one trawler, the leading vessel struck a mine. A huge hole was blown in her port bow, but she did not sink because of her size. Drifting inshore the *Passing* was taken in tow and was safely berthed in Scarborough harbour for repairs (Figure 14).

At eleven o'clock that same day, a second vessel the 273-ton

Orianda, was blown up while steaming at full speed. Unable to stop, she careered on through the sea, sinking as she took on more water. One man went down with the ship; the remainder, including skipper Lieutenant HB Boothby, RNR, abandoned ship and were rescued by a paddle steamer. Work was suspended after this until the next day, when the 203-ton trawler *Garmo* was destroyed by a mine and sunk with the loss of six lives south of Cayton Bay. On Christmas Day 1914 a third minesweeping trawler, the 287-ton *Nighthawk*, struck one of the Kolberg's mines and sank in ten seconds. Amazingly, seven of the thirteen crew were saved, largely thanks to the actions of her skipper Sub-Lieutenant W Senior, who after being in the freezing water for some time managed to reach a raft, and boarding this, he propelled it with his hands toward his shipmates who he then assisted onto the raft.

Many years later in 1973 one of the local inshore trawlers working off Scarborough fouled her nets on an underwater obstruction, and when they were hauled up a large piece of rusty steel was seen to be caught in them. Unfortunately the obstruction broke up before it could be brought on board, and part of the 'catch' fell back into the water and sank, but not before the crew had recognised their prize. They knew beyond doubt that they had trawled up a part of the bow of a steam trawler, and the piece that remained in the net was carefully examined. On the rusty steel were some brass letters which read NIGH... the rest had broken away. By an amazing coincidence they had fished up a section of the ill-fated trawler *Nighthawk*.

The next steam trawler to come to grief amid the Scarborough mine-field was Minesweeper No.450, *Banyers*. Six men perished when she blew up, but among the survivors was skipper HB Boothby who, it will be remembered, had already been blown up hereabouts a matter of weeks before. On this occasion he had escaped by climbing out through the wheelhouse window shortly before the boat sank. Like his previous command the *Orianda*, the *Banyers* was almost a new ship having only been built in 1914.

During the First World War 214 minesweepers were lost; on average one per week for the entire period of the conflict. Each time one of these vessels sank roughly half the crew died. Hull and Grimsby between them supplied around eight hundred trawlers and 9,000 men to defend their country during the 1914-18 war. Of the mines that were originally laid off Scarborough, fifty-three were swept up in a month, and by St George's Day 1915 when sweeping ceased, sixty-nine had been cleared. Sadly, many of the other mines had already served their deadly purpose, however; fourteen steamships, four minesweepers, and two patrol vessels had been sunk by them with the loss of about one hundred lives. After mine-sweeping operation had been suspended, two steam trawlers that were fishing came upon the Kolberg's mines and were sunk. The 289-ton Hull trawler *Sapphire* on 1 March 1915, and three months later the 151-ton Scarborough trawler *Condor* on 29 May. Skipper Bob Heritage and the entire crew of eight men died.

Before the menace of the Scarborough mine-field had gone, however, another threat to fishermen had already made its appearance. On 6 May 1915, the Hull steam trawler *Merrie Islington* was fishing some six miles north-east of Whitby when a German submarine surfaced close by. The crew of the vessel, all Scarborough men, were ordered at gun point to abandon ship and take to the lifeboats, whereupon the U-boat crew planted a bomb on the 147-ton *Merrie Islington* and sank her. She was the first of many fishing craft to be sunk in this manner during the course of the war. In fact, the Scarborough fleet was very nearly wiped out by U-boats in this way.

On 13 July 1916, two Scarborough steam trawlers, the *Florence* and the *Dalhousie*, were captured and sunk by U-boats approximately ten miles north-north-east of Whitby. This was only the beginning. On September 25 1916, no less than eleven Scarborough trawlers were sunk by a single U-boat some twenty miles north-east of Scarborough. Although the crews were landed safely, they had lost their means of livelihood, for by this date Scarborough was now left with only four trawlers. On the same day, six steam trawlers from other ports met the same fate in the same area, and many others suffered likewise off other parts of the Yorkshire coast.

One particularly interesting U-boat incident took place off Flamborough Head on 5 May 1917, when a number of herring cobbles were fishing the seas thereabouts. They were in fact, sticking their necks out, for they had been told not to fish that area, as it was known to be a favourite hunting ground for German submarines. However, fish was at that time in short supply and prices were good, so many skippers in their greed took the risk. On most occasions they were in fact in little danger, and tales are told of U-boat skippers actually talking to fishermen and obtaining fish from them – a request that fishermen would be unlikely to refuse!

On this occasion, however, a U-boat commander took offence at the name of one of the cobles, the 21-ton *Edith Cavell*, and ordered the crew aboard his submarine. (Edith Cavell was a British nurse

Figure 15. The Scarborough keelboat Sincere stranded south of Cayton Bay where she became a wreck, May 1968.

who was matron of a Belgian clinic, who was executed by the Germans in 1916 for assisting Allied soldiers to escape). He then sank the year-old vessel. The U-boat skipper asked one of the young apprentices where he would have been that day had he not been at sea. 'At Sunday School, sir' replied the boy. Apparently the commander was well-pleased with this answer and said, 'Then I'll see you are there next Sunday'. Eventually the crew of the *Edith Cavell* were released, along with some other prisoners, off the Faroe Islands. When the crew, all Filey men, arrived back home after some time, half the population turned up at the railway station to receive them! During their incarceration on the U-boat, they had learned that the Germans were out to attack the Scarborough craft the *Victory* whose name also had offended the U-boat skipper. So seriously was this threat taken by the authorities that the *Victory* had her name changed immediately, and as a secondary precaution, she was sent to another port for the rest of the war.

U-boats did not always have it their own way when they attacked fishing craft. Between 1917 and 1918 many trawlers were armed in order that they could defend themselves. On one occasion a number of trawlers returning from Iceland during the summer of 1918 got the better of a submarine that came upon them. Later a second group of trawlers was also attacked by a U-boat that fired two torpedoes at them, both of which missed their targets. This was unusual, as was the fact that German captains usually then surfaced to take revenge. In this instance her skipper chose not to engage in a gun battle with the trawlers. Significantly perhaps, in the third year of the war 156 trawlers were sunk by U-boats, but in the fourth year, the number fell to just four!

Altogether in the First World War, 670 fishing vessels were destroyed by enemy activity, a truly staggering figure. The Second World War brought with it yet another menace, namely attack from the air. On 17 December 1939, five trawlers were bombed off the north-east coast, and four of them sank. Strangely, the only survivor, the Hull trawler *Dromio,* was to sink five days later after being run down by an Italian vessel north of Whitby.

Air attacks on trawlers became quite commonplace, and as a result many trawlers were armed with Lewis guns. One Scarborough vessel, the steam drifter *Silver Line,* engaged in action with a German Heinkel, and the gunner Tom Watkinson drove the raider off. The Heinkel was later shot down by a British spitfire. Another steam trawler that fought back and lived to tell the tale was the *Persian Empire.* Captain Thomas Robson fired distress rockets at a German aeroplane that was attacking his craft, and although he did not harm the raider, he did cause it to drop its bombs wide of the mark.

Earlier in the Second World War, on 28 December 1939, an old hazard returned to haunt the fishing fleets around the British Isles when the Grimsby trawler *Resercho* netted a mine while fishing in Bridlington Bay. The mate said later that as they hauled the net out of the water, an explosion occurred and a sheet of flame enveloped the ship. Steam pipes ruptured, hot ashes from the boiler fires shot into the air and fell about them, and tons of seawater crashed down on the deck. But amazingly all nine crew escaped with their lives, and they were able to signal a passing steamer just before they abandoned the sinking trawler.

Since the period after the Second World War the fishing industry has changed dramatically. It had taken hundreds of years to develop the sailing trawlers that reached their peak in the 1880s, yet no sooner had that type been perfected than it was made obsolete by the advent of paddle trawlers. The paddle 'fishers' enjoyed only a brief spell of success though, and were outdated in little more than twenty years. Screw-steam fishing craft proved to be more successful; coal-burning steam-trawlers were in use for only half a century, while oil-burning vessels are still in use today. Then there was petrol and finally diesel, which is of course the most common form of engine propulsion today (Figure 15). A marine diesel engine can be drenched in water, yet will continue to run, while such treatment on other types would stop the engine in its tracks. Lastly, as in most other industries, technology came along, radar for instance, that allowed fish to be tracked more successfully, but for all that what of the future?

As more and more nations become aware of the danger of over-fishing and as fish stocks dwindle, fishing limits are being continually extended and bans imposed on the quotas allowed to be caught, thus reducing the areas left for deep sea fishermen to work in. As a result of this, they are constantly looking to new and previously untapped sources for fish and endeavouring to alter and shape our taste in fish.

In February 1974 the stern trawler *Luneda* made history when she became the first trawler to sell a catch of deep-water fish caught in the Atlantic Ocean. Previous visits had been made to these grounds on an experimental basis, but the *Luneda* was the first ship to sell an entire catch from this area. Though the response to the new kinds of fish was said to be encouraging, there is no doubt

Figure 16. Women packing herrings at Scarborough in the 1930s, just one of the traditional tasks carried out by girls. Notice the white flecks of salt on the aprons and barrels.

Figure 17. Fishermen mending crab pots alongside the quay at Scarborough, a sight still seen in many ports and harbours today.

that many people looked at them with some apprehension. Instead of cod, haddock, plaice and skate, the *Luneda* brought back grenadiers, scabbard, mora, blue-ling and gephyroberyx and faced a barrage of television cameras and newspaper reporters on her return. These fish had been caught at depths of between 200 and 700 fathoms, something that could not have been achieved until that date. Perhaps this is where the future of the industry lies – in the murky depths of the world's deepest oceans. But one thing is for sure, risk in every sense of the word, is the heritage of the fisherman today, as it always has been (Figures 16 & 17).

Notes and References

1. *The Ballad of Robin Hood,* Anon. Sixteenth century.
2. L Toulmin Smith, Editor. *The Itinerary of John Leland in or About the Years 1535-43,* Vol.1 (1907),
3. Atkinson, Rev., Whitby Chartulary, CCCLXXIV & DLXI, p311,500.
4. Burton's *Monasticon Eboracense* (1758), p226; Charlton, *History of Whitby,* (1776), p77,148-9.
5. Young, Rev. G. *History of Whitby,* Vol.2, p328.
6. Whitby Chartulary, CCLXVII & CCXCV, p212,235; Charlton, p206-7; Young, p333.
7. Charlton, *History of Whitby.*
8. The rights of the impropriator of the parish of Whitby in respect of the tithe of fish were the subject of litigation in the year 1758. (Bishop of Norwich v. Grainger. – Wood's Collection of Decrees by the Court of Exchequer in Tithe Causes, 1798, Vol.2, p540.
9. See Atton, Henry & Holland, Henry H, *The King's Custom* (1908), p12-4.
10. PRO, Exchequer, KR, Customs Accounts No.55/10.
11. According to Halliwell's *Dictionary of Archaic and Provincial Words,* a last of herrings was calculated at 20,000 fish – the following quotation being added: 'white herrings a laste, that is to saye, xij barrelles.' (Ord. And Reg. P102). The *Oxford English Dictionary* (1903) says a last of cod and herrings was formally 12 barrels, but of red herrings and pilchards 10,000 to 13,200 fish. At Whitby a last of herrings was said in 1909 to consist of 10,000 herrings, but the true number was much larger, each hundred being a customary hundred, viz. 132 herrings, or 13,200 to the 'last'.
12. PRO, Exchequer, KR, Customs Accounts No.134/2.
13. The introductory part of the proclamation (which was made by King Richard II at Hereford, on 29 August 1394) establishes that the herring fishery was, at the time, the principal Whitby industry, and is given in *Rymer's Foedera* (1728), Vol.7, p788.
14. Atkinson, Rev., *Memorials of Old Whitby,* p198.
15. Whitby Chartulary, p576-7; Young, p920,922.
16. PRO, Exchequer, KR, Customs Accounts No.49/10.
17. North Riding Quarter Sessions Records, Vol.4, p55,67,etc.
18. Kingston upon Hull Record Office, BRW/5/12, 31 October 1653.
19. *ibid.*
20. Heath, P. 'North Sea Fishing in the Fifteenth Century', *Northern History,* Vol.3, 1968, p58-61.
21. Walker, D S., *Whitby Fishing* (1968).
22. Ord, J W., *The History and Antiquities of Cleveland* (1846), p357.
23. Fisher, R., *Flamborough Village and Headland* (1894), p143.
24. *ibid.*
25. *Scarborough Gazette,* 24 September 1884.
26. Young, Rev. G., *History of Whitby,* Vol.2
27. Gaskin, Tate, *The Old Seaport of Whitby* (1909).
28. Robinson, R A., *History of the Yorkshire Coast Fishing Industry 1780-1914* (1987). Hull University Press.

6. ANDREW MARVELL – CROMWELL'S POET

by Alex Heywood

ANDREW MARVELL (1621-78), the poet of Oliver Cromwell and the Protectorate, was one of the greatest satirists England has produced. So great, indeed, that there are many who attribute his sudden death at the age of fifty-seven, to poisoning by one of the many men at whom his rapier-like pen had been directed. Yet Marvell was much more than a poet, he was a Member of Parliament, traveller, philosopher, and friend and colleague of John Milton.

Marvell was born on 31 March 1621, at Winestead, in Holderness. His father was a native of Cambridge and an MA of Emmanuel College there, which was, during his time, strongly imbued with Puritanism. It was, therefore, quite natural that the elder Marvell should enter the Church, and that he should instill into young Andrew's mind a youthful love of Calvinism. Little is known about the early years of the boy who was later to take England by storm except that he was taught initially by his father at Hull Grammar School, where the elder Marvell was headmaster as well as being a Calvinistic minister. At the age of fifteen, Andrew Marvell was admitted to Trinity College, Cambridge, where he remained for four years, until 1640, when his father died. The next ten years in his life are obscure, although it is known that he spent four of them abroad (1642-46), travelling in Italy, Spain, France and Holland, possibly using money from an inheritance. It was in Rome that he first met John Milton, who was already a poet not merely of promise, but of high achievement, and who by this date already had strong opinions about the Church and State. Yet whether Marvell ever went the full length of Milton's beliefs is not very evident, but it is likely he did not for Andrew seems to have been a much more cautious man in many aspects of his life.

By 1649, Andrew Marvell was back in England, for two of his poems where published during that year: one as a preface to a book of poetry by Richard Lovelace, and the other in a collection issued on the death of Lord Hastings. The poem to Lovelace, together with other early works, show that his sympathies at this date were with the Royalist cause; and that he judged the Civil War between Cromwell and the King as a spectator, and not as a partisan. For some time he was tutor to the daughter of Lord Fairfax, during which period he wrote his pastoral and garden verses.

In 1650, Milton, who was by now totally blind, wrote to Lord Bradshaw, chief of the regicide judges, recommending that Marvell be appointed his assistant in the Secretaryship for Foreign Tongues. Andrew was unsuccessful despite the high praise given by Milton. Possibly this was a blessing in disguise, for within a matter of weeks of his being rejected, he was chosen as tutor to Oliver Cromwell's ward, William Dutton, and went with him to live at Eton. On 28 July, Marvell reported favourably to Cromwell on the progress of his pupil, and the Protector replied in appreciative terms. It was in this year also, that Marvell wrote his *Horatian Ode upun Cromwell's Return from Ireland* that also, interestingly and perhaps daringly, reflected his warmest sympathies for King Charles I (Figure 1).

Figure 1. King Charles I

Throughout his tutorship, Andrew Marvell maintained his ambitions and friendship with Milton who sent him in 1654, a copy of his famous second defence of the people of England, and Andrew in his letter of thanks to the blind poet, described the work as:

...a Trajan's column, in whose willing ascent we see embossed the several monuments of your learned victories.

Three years later, Andrew Marvell was at last appointed Milton's assistant at a salary of £200 a year, and he went to live in Whitehall, where he was provided with accommodation by the Council of State.

During his first year in the office of the Foreign Tongues Secretaryship, he published his celebrated poem, *The First Anniversary of the Government under His Highness the Lord Protector* and, in it he showed tremendous admiration for Cromwell. Very soon, he became recognised as Oliver Cromwell's poet, for nearly every verse he composed at that period, was in praise of the government, and many were addressed personally to the Protector. In November 1657, he wrote two pastoral songs in celebration of the wedding of Mary Cromwell and in these Cromwell appeared as Jove himself. A month later he described, in another fine poem, the victory of Blake at Santa Cruz; but, once again, the work was addressed to the Protector himself. The long series of Cromwellian poems ended with *Upon the Death of his late Highness the Lord Protector* (d.1658), and here great personal sincerity and grief are clearly shown.

Andrew Marvell (Figure 2) gave the same unswerving support to Oliver Cromwell's third son, Richard (1626-1712) and, in fact, in order to render even greater service, entered Parliament as Member for Hull in 1659. Of Richard, Marvell wrote, a Cromwell, in an hour a prince will grow. Later, Richard Cromwell who succeeded his father in September 1658 as Lord Protector, was to dissolve Parliament in 1659 and recall a Rump Parliament similar to that of 1653. Unfortunately, he found the task of ruling beyond him, and was forced to abdicate in May 1659. The end of Cromwellian rule left the way open for the return of King Charles II (Figure 3).

Figure 2. A portrait of Andrew Marvell. Courtesy of the Trustees of the national Portrait Gallery

In spite of his admiration for the Cromwell family, however, Marvell never disapproved of the recall of the monarch; and his devotion to Cromwell did not appear to stand in his way, for he was re-elected MP for Hull in April 1660 and again a year later. At that period, Hull maintained the custom of paying its Member of Parliament, and Marvell and his colleague, Anthony Gilbert, received 6s 8d a day for so long as the sessions of the House of Commons sat (Figure 4). It is also clear that Andrew attended to his Parliamentary duties assiduously and that he kept in close touch with his constituents, for he wrote no fewer than three hundred letters to them giving information on what had transpired in Parliament. At that time, it should be remembered the publication of debates was strictly forbidden; and these letters, many of which are still preserved at Hull, were the only means of letting the people know just what was going on in the House of Commons. Another interesting feature of these Parliamentary despatches was that Marvell scarcely ever spoke of himself.

Andrew appears to have made an important place for himself in the court of King Charles, for in June 1663, he was appointed to accompany Charles Howard, first Earl of Carlisle, in his embassy to

Figure 4. The House of Commons, from an engraving by John Glover

Figure 3. King Charles II

Russia, Sweden and Denmark. He dutifully wrote to the Corporation of Hull saying:

> *It is no new thing for Members of our House to be dispensed with, for the service of the King and the nation in foreign parts. And you may be sure I will not stir without special leave of the House, so that you may be freed from any possibility of being importuned or tempted to make any other choice in my absence.*

Although his trip was scheduled to last for twelve months only, he did not return to England until the beginning of 1665, when he found that Parliament was sitting at Oxford because of the plague then raging in the capital. He voted consistently with the government, and helped to pass numerous Bills, full details of which he sent regularly to his constituents in Hull.

The autumn of 1666 brought the Great Fire of London that in its wake purged the capital of the plague. Andrew Marvell informed the people of Hull that Parliament was to return to London to transact business of a mainly financial nature.

Although Andrew's Parliamentary correspondence with his constituents at Hull, continued without interruption between the years 1667 and 1670, it threw no light at all on his own ideas; nor did it tell anything of his personal character. Rarely did he even venture to give an opinion on any subject, unless it was in the direct interests of his constituents, as the following extracts from his letters show:

> ***December 22, 1666:*** *Today the Duke of Buckingham and Marquis of Dorchester were, upon their petitions, released from the Tower, having been committed for quarrelling and scuffling the other day when we were at the Canary Conference.*

> ***February 9, 1667:*** *I am sorry to hear of several fires of late in your town, but by God's mercy prevented from doing much harm. Though I know your vigilance, and have been informed of the occasions, I cannot but, out of the earnestness of mine own sense, advise you to have a careful eye against all such accidents. We have had so much of them here in the South that it makes me almost superstitious. But indeed, as sometimes there arise new diseases, so there are seasons of more particular judgements, such as that of fires seem of late to have been upon this nation.*

> ***July 25, 1667:*** *Yesternight, at one o'clock, a very dangerous fire happened in Southwark, but by blowing up the next house in good time, there was but twelve consumed or ruined. Cannot but advise you to have especial care in your own town of any such accident or what*

you will call it; for I am sorry we can yet see no clearer by so many lights.

October 25, 1667: *This morning several members of our House did in their places move the House to proceed to an impeachment against the Earl of Clarendon and laid very high crimes to his charge.*

November 14, 1667: *Rarely the business of the House hath been of late so earnestly daily, and so long, that I have not had the time, and scarce vigour left me by night to write to you. The Earl of Clarendon has taken up much of our time till within these three days. But since his impeachment hath been carried up to the House of Lords we have some leisure from that.*

November 23, 1667: *The Lords and we cannot yet get off the difficulties risen between us on occasion of our House s demanding the Earl of Clarendon's imprisonment upon a general charge of treason.*

December 3, 1667: *The Lords yesterday sent a message by Judge Archer and Judge Morton that, upon the whole matter, they were not satisfied to commit the Earl of Clarendon without particular cause specified or assigned; whereupon our House, after very long debate, voted that the Lords not comply with the desires of the House of Commons in committing and sequestering from their House the Earl of Clarendon, upon the impeachment carried up against him, is an obstruction of the public justice in the proceedings of both houses of Parliament, and is the precedent of evil and dangerous consequences. Today the Lords sent down another message to us, that they had today received a large petition from the Earl of Clarendon, intimating that he has withdrawn. Hereupon our House forthwith address his Majesty that care might be taken for securing all the sea-ports lest he should pass there. I suppose he will not trouble you ate Hull.*

Marvell seems to have written to Hull approximately once a week, describing new Bills brought forward. It is clear that he attended the debates in the Commons regularly, although there is no record of him ever having taken part in any one.

He had considerable political influence, but this was due much more to his writing than to any action he took in Parliament, and his satires show how his own political opinions developed. In 1667, the year Milton gave the world *Paradise Lost* (Figure 5 & 6), he attacked the Earl of Clarendon and the court party in one of his most biting works; in the year 1672, he declared that King Charles, with all his faults, was better than his brother; by 1674, he had discovered that the King's character was the reason for the misgovernment of England, for one man's weakness a whole nation bleeds; and a year later Marvell was demanding the end of the reign of the House of Stuart, and the substitution of a republic, patterned on Rome. Of course, these outspoken satires were printed and circulated in secret, but on one important subject he was able to write openly and for a wide audience, and it was this which first established Andrew, throughout the country, as a political satirist of the first order.

In 1672 and 1673 he published, under his own name, the two parts of his brilliant *Rehearsal Transposed*, in which he assailed the oppressive ecclesiastical policy which was then gaining ground, under the direction of Samuel Parker, Bishop of Oxford, the leading champion of intolerance. The main target for his satire was, of course, Bishop Parker himself whom Marvell ridiculed so much that he and his party were finally humbled. Even Charles II read *Rehearsal Transposed* with so much enjoyment, that when he was asked to suppress the second edition, he declared:

I will not have it suppressed for Parker has done me wrong and this man Marvell has done me right.

Encouraged and perhaps emboldened by his astounding success, Marvell wrote a number of other essays relating to the religious controversy, and these earned for him the reputation of a great wit, even in court. Loving ridicule for its own sake, he cared not whether his pen smote friend or foe, Church or Conventicle. He was described as:

... the liveliest droll of the age, whose books are the delight of all classes from the King to the tradesmen.

No measures were omitted by the various parties and factions in attempting to win over Andrew Marvell. He was threatened; he was flattered; he was thwarted; he was caressed; he was courted by beauties, but no Delilah could discover the secret of his strength. His own integrity was proof against corruption, and he never succumbed to the wiles of those who sought to buy him, in spite of the fact that he was far from affluent, and living in an age when brilliant writers were abysmally paid, and when the

Figure 5. Title page to the first edition of Paradise Lost

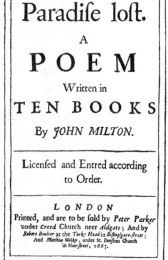

Figure 6. Title page to the second edition of Paradise Lost

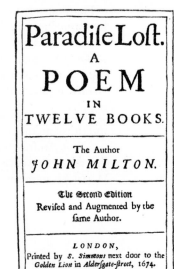

copyright of *Paradise Lost* was sold for fifteen pounds.

Early in 1677, he published his *Extraordinary Black Book*, which contained some of the most licentious comments that even he had dared to make. Fortunately for him, and unfortunately for the people about whom he wrote, there were no laws of libel in those days, such as we know now. If there had been, then Marvell would have been found guilty of the most gross criminal libel imaginable, for these are some of the things he said, under the heading, A List of the Principal Labourers in the Great Design of Popery.

Sir Charles Harbour, surveyor-general, has got £100,000 of the King and the kingdom: he was formerly a solicitor of Staples Inn, till lewdness and poverty brought him to court.

Sir Capelston Bamfield, Baronet, much addicted to tippling, presented to the King by his pretended wife, Betty Roberts.

Sir Winston Churchill, was a commissioner of the court of claims in Ireland, now one of the clerks of the green cloth. He proffered his own daughter to the Duke of York, and has got in boons £10,000.

Sir John Holmes, Sir Ross's brother, a cowardly, baffled sea-captain, twice boxed and once whipped with a dog whip, as many gentlemen can testify: chosen in the night without head officer of the town and but one burgess, yet voted well-elected this last session.

Samuel Pepys, once a tailor, then serving man to the Lord Sandwich, now secretary to the Admiralty, got by passes and other illegal wages £40,000.

Sir William Bassett, Henry Seymour s son-in-law, has £1,000 given him by Clifford: he has a promise of place in the law: always drunk when he can get money.

To crown all, Marvell wrote, in an introduction to the *Black Book*, what was perhaps his most damaging satire of all, for he said:

The author begs pardon of those gentlemen here named, if he has, for want of better information, under-valued the price and merit of their voices, which shall be ready, upon their advertisement, to amend; but more particularly he must beg the excuse of many more gentlemen, no less deserving, whom he hath omitted, not out of any malice or for want of good will, but of timely notice.

Publication of his book produced a sensation; but it amused the King and those members of court who were not mentioned in it. The result was that Andrew's company was constantly sought by the great as well as by the witty, and he was even admitted to the company of the Merry Monarch himself, and was on terms of close friendship with

Prince Rupert. But sadly, he became too sure of himself; and, towards the end of 1677, when he was fifty-six and at the height of his career as a satirist, he published his *Account of the growth of Popery and Arbitrary Government in England,* ostensibly printed in Amsterdam. It reviewed the reign of the King from the time of the long prorogation of November 1675, and claimed to prove that there was a design to change the lawful government of England into an absolute tyranny, and to convert the established Protestant religion into downright Popery. Though issued without his name, it was readily recognised as his work, and the *London Gazette* announced that the government offered a reward of £100 for the discovery of the author, and even greater rewards were offered privately. The campaign to discover the author of the several seditious and scandalous libels accelerated as the weeks went by.

So little was Marvell himself concerned about the attention, that he wrote to a friend in terms of jocular defiance. The letter was dated 10 June 1678, and is the last of his writings in existence:

> *There came out, about Christmas last, a large book concerning The Growth of Popery and Arbitrary Government . There have been great rewards offered to any who would inform of the author. Three or four books, printed since, have described, as near as it was proper to go, the man, Mr Marvell, as being a Member of Parliament, to have been the author...*

No prosecution took place, but legal punishment was by no means the worst thing that a critical and satirical writer had to fear. His life had been threatened during his controversy with Bishop Parker, and now he had to hide for days on end because of the way in which he was menaced yet again. He even fled from London to his constituency at Hull (Figure 7), for in the records of Hull

Figure 7. View of Hull in the seventeenth century from Hollar's engraving, 1640

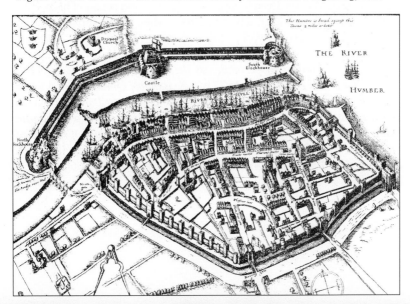

Corporation this notice appears:

This day, July 29, 1678, the court being met, Andrew Marvell, Esq, one of the burgesses of Parliament for this borough, came into court and several discourses were held about the town affairs.

Eventually, Marvell was able to return to the capital, where, without any sign of illness, he died suddenly on 16 August in circumstances that have given rise to the reports that he had been poisoned, when in fact, it was undoubtedly due to the stubborn ignorance of his physician.

It was, perhaps, a singular coincidence that the Parliament in which he had sat for so long, and itself the longest to serve under the monarchy, should survive Andrew Marvell by only a single session. It was dissolved on 30 December 1678.

Marvell was probably the last Member of Parliament to receive wages from his constituents although, at later dates, others tried, unsuccessfully, to sue their boroughs for arrears.

Description of Andrew Marvell's appearance vary from authority to authority, but John Aubrey, who knew him well, wrote: he was of middling stature, pretty strong set, roundish cheeked, hazel-eyed, brown haired. In his conversation he was modest and of very few words. He was wont to say he would not drink high or freely with anyone with whom he could not trust his life.

Very few of Marvell's poems were published during his lifetime, and most of those that were, were mainly the products of his youth and early manhood. Yet while they have a great deal of over-activity of fancy and remoteness of allusion, many of them also have a heart-felt tenderness and a childish simplicity of feeling that atone for their conceits. The first collected works of his were published in 1680-81, but this edition was by no means complete, and it was not until 1765 that a comprehensive collection was produced by Thomas Hollis, who also wrote a life of Marvell. Even today, it is difficult to find copies of his poems, which varied almost as much in quality as they did in subject matter.

Of Marvell's prose works, his two-part volume, *The Rehearsal Transposed*, is outstanding, but the following are also important: *A Seasonable Argument to persuade all the Grand Juries of England to petition for a new Parliament* (1677); *A Seasonable Question and a useful Answer contained in an exchange of a Letter between a Parliament Man in Cornwall and a Bencher of the Temple* (1676); *A Letter from a Parliament Man to his Friend concerning the proceedings of the House of Commons* (1675); a translation of *Suetonius* in 1672; and of course, *Account of the growth of Popery and Arbitrary Government in England* (1677).

7. The Smugglers Revenge

by Peter Howorth

SALT PANS is little more than an indentation on the coast some five miles north of Scarborough (Figure 1). It is about one mile from the village of Cloughton, to the north of Cloughton Wyke, on the rocky coast of North Yorkshire (Figure 2). On the night of Sunday, 20 August 1820, a lugger from Flushing in Holland successfully rendezvoused with the local smugglers and landed about two hundred tubs of gin and a quantity of tea and tobacco.

The smugglers may have been observed. The Revenue Officers were later to produce informants, who claimed to have witnessed the landing and to have recognised some of the smugglers involved, as the goods were moved away from the landing area. The following day the authorities were able to seize 115 tubs of gin, which were still

Figure1. The coastline near Burniston and Cloughton in 1772 showing Salt Pans.

Figure 2. Salt Pans, on the rocky coast near Burniston and Cloughton.

concealed among the rocks, and attempted 'to rescue' a boy who was found guarding them. Not surprising perhaps, the boy appears to have preferred not to wait until rescued. A tub, or anker, held about eight and a half gallons of spirits, so that the seizure represented just under one thousand gallons of gin, but none of the smugglers were caught in the act.

In a tight, close-knit community such as the fishing community of Scarborough, virtually confined to a handful of crowded streets, the identity of the smugglers and their supporters could not be kept a secret for long, but that did not make the task of the Revenue Officers an easy one. Smuggling was widespread at that date and widely accepted (Figure 3). High rates of duty on imports, cumbersome regulations on trade practices and a high demand for the goods, all encouraged smuggling and ensured that it was a popular and profitable enterprise, supported by many in all ranks of society.

In the face of such support, gathering evidence against the smugglers and persuading witnesses to stand up in court, was a daunting task. The authorities were heavily dependent upon informers. The going rate of payment to these persons was anything from twenty to fifty pounds, but in addition, the Revenue Officers took care to look after their informants in a variety of ways. Such methods were proving very successful in the Scarborough area in 1820. The *Hull Advertiser* when reporting the Salt Pans landing noted

Figure 3. A revenue cutter in pursuit of a smuggler's vessel off the Yorkshire coast.

that a great number of the smugglers in the neighbourhood had been convicted lately, with heavy penalties. However, just as the identity of smugglers was common knowledge to many, some people had a shrewd idea of who was doing the informing. William Mead, of Burniston, was widely believed to be the leader of a group that regularly supplied information to the authorities. One witness was later to put the matter succinctly, 'There has been a deal of information. Mead has told many tales about smuggling, as people say.'

In the aftermath of the Salt Pans landing, Mead informed the Revenue Officers that he had been present at the place at about eleven o'clock that night and seen James Law and his son-in-law, John Scott, lead three horses loaded with twenty-one half-ankers of gin and two bales of tobacco from the beach. No less than eight other informants came forward to confirm this and name others involved. If they were all telling the truth, Salt Pans must have been a crowded venue that August evening.

The Revenue Officers, acting on the information received, arrested Law and the others named, with the exception of John Scott, who fled when the officers came to take him. The Attorney-General duly filed 'an information' against six individuals on smuggling charges; cases which were tried in the Exchequer in London, a court far removed from local interests and sympathetic juries. Mead and the other informants gave their evidence at the trials and all the smugglers were found guilty, except James Law, who was acquitted.

It was this acquittal that was to spark off a train of events over three years, which was to involve hundreds of people rioting in the streets of Scarborough, lead to several trials and was to culminate in the longest Assize case at York that anyone could ever recall.

James Law was described as a respectable farmer who lived in Staintondale, just north of Cloughton. He was according to one girl, 'not an old man, nor a young one'. She thought he might not be sixty years of age. He had been convicted of smuggling in 1818 and was regularly found in the company of other known smugglers. His actions following the acquittal were obviously based on a desire for revenge. Yet whether it was because Law was genuinely innocent in this instance and had been 'fitted-up' by Mead, or whether his acquittal provided the opportunity for the smugglers to try and reduce Mead's influence and activities against the gang, cannot be known. Either way, his response was to present eighteen indictments for perjury against William Mead and others who had given evidence at his trial. The Grand Jury at the Quarter Sessions decided that there was a case to answer and the matter was transferred to the Court of King's Bench.

Law's move was a bold one. As the trials would be held in London, Law and his supporters would be faced with the expense of taking their witnesses to the capital for several days, as well as meeting the legal costs of a series of trials. It was later to be claimed that the costs came to £5,000. Much of this was raised before the trials by subscription in the Scarborough area, a further sign of public support and, perhaps, a pointer that Law was not acting alone. The first perjury case against Mead came before the court in December 1822.

James Law was not the only person seeking revenge on the informants. In a case that was intertwined with that of Law, John Dodsworth, a farmer from Harwood Dale in Hackness, claimed that two men, Thomas Scott and William Bradbury, had broken into his dairy in November 1821 and stolen three butter firkins. They had sold them to Jonathan Bailey for three pounds. Both Scott and Bailey had been prosecution witnesses at the smugglers' trial. Dodsworth had not brought any charges until August 1822, because Bradbury had been imprisoned in York Castle until that date (Figure 4). When released, he had confessed to Dodsworth and implicated Scott and Bailey in the robbery. He was to be the main prosecution witness.

When the case finally came to court in March 1823, it was to last a whole day, an unusual length of time for that period in history.

Figure 4. An aerial view of York Castle in 1928 showing the prison at the top to the right of Cliffords Tower and the rear of the Assize Court at the bottom.

Dodsworth was cross-examined for over two hours by defence counsel. He had to admit that he was soon to face smuggling charges and that he had been in London to give evidence against William Mead in the perjury trials and that Scott had been there on the other side. He was then asked if he did not expect Scott to be a witness against him in the forthcoming Exchequer trial. 'The question was put to him nearly a hundred times and in various forms, but he contrived to elude it, by fencing most ingeniously and it was not 'til his Lordship seriously admonished him on the consequences of prevarication that he directly stated that he knew Scott to be a witness for the Crown.'

The key witness for the prosecution was William Bradbury. He had spent time in the House of Correction at Beverley and Northallerton and two periods in York Castle. His evidence was that Scott had approached him to rob the farmer Dodsworth and that Bailey had agreed to buy the stolen goods from them. On being released from prison Bradbury said he felt compelled to confess his part. Both he and Dodsworth were closely cross-examined over payments should Scott be convicted. Dodsworth denied making any promises to Bradbury and the defence failed to show that money he had been given whilst in prison was from Dodsworth.

Scott's defence was that the prosecution had been brought out of spite and malice and because he had given evidence against the smugglers. The constable of Whitby testified that on the slow journey to York Castle to await trial, the two prisoners had quarrelled most of the way. Scott had reproached Bradbury for swearing falsely against him and was told that if he had not testified in London, Bradbury would not have informed against him.

The Judge's summing-up left little room for misinterpretation. He pointed out the equivocation, contradictions and inconsistent conduct of many of the witnesses for the prosecution. This might well be a conspiracy to injure the prisoners. Against Jonathan Bailey, in his opinion, there was no satisfactory evidence and he left it to the jury to say, under all the circumstances, whether the proof against Scott was sufficiently conclusive.

The jury took just forty-five minutes to acquit Bailey and find Scott guilty. The Judge 'received the verdict with surprise and told the jury it was a very different one from what the evidence had led him to expect'.

That verdict in March 1823 can, perhaps, only be understood against events that go back to the perjury trials in December of the previous year and before. It had taken an hour to empanel a jury to try the unfortunate Scott, but it would appear improbable that the jury was not influenced by the background to the trial and was not caught up in the general excitement of events in Scarborough at that period.

There were over one hundred partisan Yorkshiremen in London in December 1822 in support of the parties at the perjury trials, the first of which centred on William Mead's evidence against James Law. Mr Jones, who had defended Law in the original smuggling trial, now led for the prosecution, 'an exception to the usual habits of his professional life.' He was instructed by the Scarborough solicitor, Mr Page, who appears to have been the preferred choice of smugglers in the district. Against them as Jones was to point out, was 'all the power of the Crown seemed put forth to protect the defendant'. Leading the formidable array of counsel on the opposing side were the Attorney-General and the Solicitor-General. The case was tried before Lord Chief Justice Abbot, and all-in-all the scene must have been a daunting one for many of the witnesses.

The basis of the case against Mead was that Law, who lived quite near to Salt Pans, had been away from home at the time of the landings. The informants had used this knowledge to concoct a story against him and Scott, his son-in-law. Jones then proceeded to outline Law's movements on the night. He had, as usual for Sunday, been to chapel and had ridden back as far as Scalby with the vicar. He had then called at another house to drink tea with friends until ten o'clock at night, before returning to his own home with two further acquaintances. Together they had prepared a cartload of wool, which he was taking to Pickering. He produced a succession of witnesses to confirm these events.

Scott, who denied having run away to avoid arrest, had been ill on that night in August 1820, and had gone to bed early. His wife could confirm this, but she could not at that time leave their young children to travel to London to give evidence.

The Solicitor-General for Mead, argued that the account of events was largely irrelevant. There was no need to dispute the visit to church, nor that Law had been drinking tea afterwards, but the house where he had been at ten o'clock was very close to Salt Pans and new witnesses had been discovered since the trial, who could confirm the presence of Law and Scott at the landing.

The Lord Chief Justice confirmed what was obvious to all. 'It was painful for him to say, that on one side or the other, there must have been very wilful and abundant perjury.' He left it to the jury to say which side was lying. After deliberating for two hours, the jury reached the conclusion that William Mead was guilty of perjury.

Law's triumph was short lived. If the supply of information against the smugglers was not to dry up, Mead had to be protected. The following day, Friday 20 December, when the second charge of perjury against Mead came before the court, the defence applied for a Special Jury. This entailed empanelling a jury formed from persons with a higher property qualification than the normal jury, in essence, jurors with a higher social standing. Court officials kept lists of special jurors, who were financially retained to attend the courts and serve as necessary.

When the names of the Special Jury were called, only five answered. This was not an uncommon event and was normally answered by a legal procedure known as 'praying a tales'; that is to move for a writ to summon sufficient additional jurors to make up the full number. It was usually a mere formality. When the Lord Chief Justice asked the defence, having asked for a Special Jury, to 'pray a tales', the Solicitor-General declined to do so. Jones, for the prosecution, protested bitterly. 'As he had not the Attorney-General's warrant,' (again normally a formality) 'he could not pray-a-tales'. To postpone the trials after Law had incurred considerable costs of nearly £5,000, would result in great hardship. He urged the Judge to force the defence to pray a tales and thus proceed with the trial. Abbot refused to do so. 'He had no power to force a defendant to pray a tales, or go to trial against their own judgement.' When the defence lawyers continued to refuse, the cases were put off until the next legal term.

James Law had every reason to feel bitter. If he felt he had been framed in his original trial, he had every justification for feeling that he had been unfairly treated in the capital. It was unlikely that the money to bring the prosecution witnesses to London and to meet the legal costs involved, could ever be raised again. Even if he pursued the case, there was no guarantee that the same strategy would not be employed against him a second time, for there was the distinct suspicion that steps had been taken to ensure that the Special Jurymen had not been available. As we shall see Law was not alone in his suspicions. To all intents and purposes, the perjury cases were at an end and the defendants would go free.

If Law felt that this was the worst that could happen, he was in for a further shock. Following the 'extraordinary exercise of discretional power by the law officers of the Crown',[1] in preventing Mead and his fellow informants coming to trial, the Solicitor-General moved for a new trial in the case where Mead had been found guilty of perjury. He asked that the verdict be set aside on two grounds. One, the jury's

Figure 5. Burniston before 1930. The house in the photograph was the southernmost dwelling in the village before houses were built alongside shortly after this picture.

verdict had been against the weight of evidence, and secondly, that he had newly sworn affidavits to support Mead. One was made by a witness who had bought several tubs of spirits from Law on the night of the landing and a second was by a Pickering man, who had been told by James Law that he had been on a run the night before. After listening to the arguments, Lord Chief Justice Abbot granted a new trial and Mead was released to return to his home at Burniston (Figure 5) on bail of five hundred pounds in his own name and two other sureties of two hundred and fifty pounds. Law had every justification for feeling that he had been 'stitched-up!'

The case received much attention. *The Times*, an anti-government newspaper at this date, felt 'it almost exceeds credibility' that the officers of the Crown should 'both move for the special jury and refuse the tales'. It believed it was the first time since the 1688 Revolution that such an event had taken place, 'thus depriving the injured person of all power to bring his injuries before a court of justice'. It also raised the question of the cost of trials. 'Why is the country to fee a Counsel for the men prosecuted... in these cases? Above all, why is the country to fee such a phalanx of lawyers? There are five barristers employed in each of the eighteen cases.'

These criticisms were linked to a fierce attack on the special jury system, which allowed large numbers 'to live very comfortably and happily upon their trade and calling of special jurymen'. Once on the

Figure 6. William Mead's house as it is today. This is the oldest house in Burniston.

list and retained at five or six guineas a week, 'these men will naturally be inclined to a verdict for the Crown. These people are well known to the officers of the court, who select the jury... I fancy they are known to the judge, between whom and themselves that sort of intimacy grows, which disposes them to listen to his lordship's dictations and constructions with great complacency.' Such criticisms began to have political overtones. The *York Courant*, perhaps the paper with the widest circulation in Yorkshire, reprinted these views with approval.[2]

If the reaction to the perjury cases was one of surprise in London, it was one of outright fury in Scarborough. An effigy of Lord Chief Justice Abbot, dressed in a gown, was carried through the streets and burnt, whilst the shutters of Mead's house at Burniston were broken and split open. On 26 January 1823, the authorities dispatched a troop of the 2nd Dragoons (The Queen's Bays) from York to Whitby to assist the Revenue Officers. A second troop was sent to Scarborough. It is probable that this reflected the concern of the local Revenue Officers, who were undoubtedly facing open hostility. Coulson, the Whitby Collector, supplied William Mead with a brace of pistols with which to defend himself.

The anger did not die down quickly and was to reach an ugly

climax on Thursday 13 February. Thursday was Market Day in Scarborough, and on that date, John Dobson, a woodman from nearby Gowland was in town. He had spent the morning at the house of Maw, the Scarborough Revenue Officer, and then gone on to the *Globe Inn*. He was later to deny that he had ever had subsistence money from Maw, or that he had told the landlord at the *Globe Inn* that Maw would pay his bill, but he had accepted that he personally had not paid it and that he did not know who had.

When Dobson left the *Globe Inn* at 1.30pm in the afternoon, he unfortunately met James Law and a group of supporters coming from the *Talbot Inn*. Dobson gave evidence that Law had told him that if 'my friend Mead (was) along with me, we should neither of us go home alive'. It was then that John Dobson was kicked to the ground and dragged in all directions. One of the group, John Watson, a convicted smuggler, urged, 'Damn him, kill him. He's an informing rascal.' Law, no doubt expressing the frustration he had felt since London, was reported to have said, 'It is no use prosecuting the Crown's evidence; we will give them the club law at home'.

The unfortunate Dobson was knocked about for an hour then taken to a pump where he was placed in the trough and had water poured on him, whilst others threw all manner of filth at him and beat him with a stick or whip. Soaked to the skin on a freezing February day, Dobson came round from semi-consciousness to find himself bound hand and foot to a ladder, which was being carried through the streets. Not surprisingly, he could recollect little of the afternoon's events, but he believed the mob were taking him 'down to the sea to drown me'. He was rescued by men who found him covered in blood that was running down his face. Ann Dawson, a girl who had once worked for Mead as a servant, went to Burniston and told him of Dobson's treatment at the hands of the smugglers.

James Law and John Dodsworth, the Harwood Dale farmer, were in the *Talbot Inn* from six o'clock in the evening until after midnight. Dodsworth was later to claim that 'I had got a little liquor (in me), but I was not fresh', but it is probably significant that when they came to ride home, Mrs Hutchinson, the landlady of the *Talbot Inn*, sent John Watson to accompany them. He rode behind William Hineson, Dodsworth's servant, as the four men travelled northwards out of Scarborough on a direct road which took them past William Mead's house in Burniston (Figures 6 & 7).

It was 2.00am before they reached that point. The quartet denied calling at Slightholme Robinson's alehouse, but witnesses in the village claimed that they had been awakened by a great racket and that the men were there for twenty minutes, calling the publican up in a very rough manner, before they moved further up the road to Adam Calvert's inn, to demand 'some more drink'. Not surprisingly, Calvert 'would not get up'. By this time many persons along the road had been awakened and lay listening to the men and horses, as they made their way through the village.

William Mead's house, a shop, lay at the top of Burniston village. It was fronted by a pavement some two or three feet wide, and raised about three feet above the roadway (Figure 7). It was later to be argued whether a horse could have mounted the raised causeway at that point. Mead, his wife, and eleven-year-old daughter Dorothy lay in one bed in the upstairs room. A friend, Robert Belt, was asleep in another bed in the same room. Next door, separated from them by only a thin and holed partition, dividing what had once been one house, lay Elizabeth Jennison and her mother, sharing a bed because Mrs Jennison's husband was away.

They were all awakened by the noise from the four smugglers as

Figure 7. A drawing of the murder of James Law outside Mead's house in Burniston. *From the York Courant*

1. *Mead's House at Burniston, February, 1823.*
2. *The window from which the pistol was fired.*
3. *Mr. Jennison's House.*
4. *Mr. Law.*
5. *Mr. Duckworth.*
6. *Watson and Hinson.*

they stopped beneath Mead's window. Amid the shouting, John Watson began to sing 'a party song', one of triumph concerning William Mead's perjuries and his conviction. After about three or four minutes, Elizabeth Jennison said she heard the sound of breaking glass from next door and the noise of gunfire. It transpired that Mead had shot at James Law who was hit in the shoulder, and the ball travelling down lodged in his chest. Law was taken to Dodsworth's house at Harwood Dale and died there a week later on 24 February 1823.

In the aftermath of the shooting, two of Mead's neighbours, a father and son, Thomas and George Brown, left Burniston with Robert Belt. They all reached the house of Mead's brother at Staintondale about 5.00am, on their way to Whitby. The youngster, George Brown, was to prove an important witness at the subsequent trial of William Mead. Mead appears to have acted with great coolness following the shooting, going back to bed and claiming not to have heard the pounding of the Scarborough constable on his door until it was broken open with a sledge-hammer. He offered no resistance, willingly produced the brace of pistols and allowed himself to be taken off in handcuffs, along with his wife and daughter, to Scarborough, where he was confined in irons in the Poor House there.

News of the incident quickly spread through the town and surrounding countryside, helped by John Watson, who walked through Scarborough wearing Law's top coat, complete with bullet hole and blood. He wore it, he said at the trial, to keep himself warm as he had no coat of his own, but he agreed that he freely admitted it was the late James Law's and did not discourage anyone from examining the garment as he wandered about the streets.

The town was still at fever pitch on Saturday, 15 February when William Mead asked William Dawson to go to Burniston to collect a box and a trunk of his belongings and bring them back to Scarborough. Dawson was the father of Anne Dawson, the girl who had told Mead of the attack on Dobson in Scarborough. Indeed, Dawson had been deeply involved in events from the beginning. He had spent four or five weeks in London before the perjury trials, though he did not appear as a witness. 'Mr Maw [the Scarborough Revenue Officer] asked me to go and I went.' He thought he might have received seventy pounds in expenses for going. He kept a lodging house in Scarborough with his four daughters, though opposing counsel at the trial were to insinuate that it was a brothel.

Dawson hired a porter called Tindall to drive a cart to Burniston for Mead's belongings. As the two men returned to Scarborough, they were stopped by John Watson and two other men on horseback. Watson was furious with Dawson and made threats. Having then made his point, he turned and with his companions rode into Scarborough for assistance, crying that 'they had got another rebel!' William Dawson, well aware of what had happened to Dobson, ran from the cart and tried to make his escape across the fields, but was soon chased by a mob of over two hundred, who caught up with him, dragged him back over the fields and then along the road into town, pelting him with stones and mud all the while. Dawson was finally rescued by one of the town officers, but took eight days to recover from his injuries. It is said that Grace Dawson, a daughter, did not recognise her father when he was brought home.

There were other violent disturbances. The house of Maw, the Revenue Officer was stoned. There was a riot in Burniston and more violence in Scarborough that led the magistrates to swear in seventeen Special Constables, seven of them from the Preventive Service. The Commissioners of Customs posted rewards of one hundred pounds to be paid for information leading to the conviction of those involved,[3] but feelings continued to run high (Figure 8). The jury at the inquest of James Law returned a verdict of 'wilful murder' by Mead and Belt, whilst 1500 people attended Scalby Church to witness Law's burial and to hear the verses of the derogatory song about William Mead sung over the grave. When Mead and Belt were transferred to York castle to await trial, they were given a military escort as far as Whitwell-on-the-Hill.

Those engaged in smuggling were quick to take advantage of the situation to cause confusion. Apart from the verses, which were printed up in Driffield and sold in Whitby and

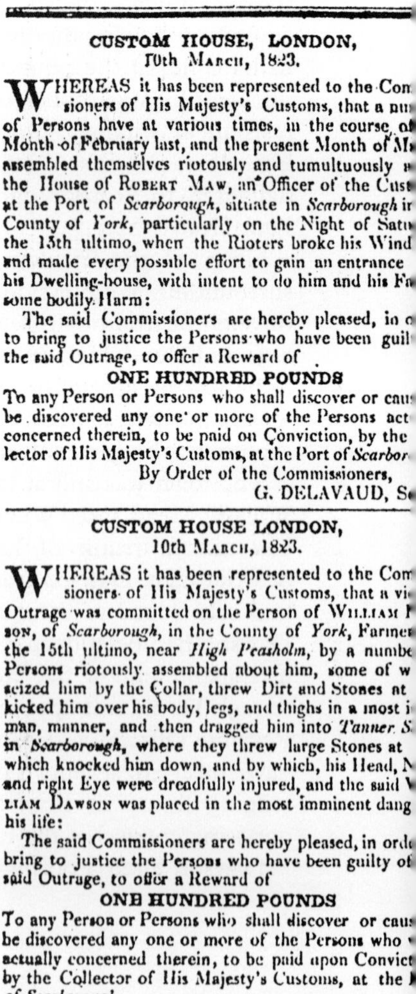

Figure 8. Reward notices posted in the newspaper after the Scarborough riots in 1823.

CUSTOM HOUSE, LONDON,
10th March, 1823.

WHEREAS it has been represented to the Com
ˑsioners of His Majesty's Customs, that a num
of Persons have at various times, in the course of
Month of February last, and the present Month of Ma
assembled themselves riotously and tumultuously a
the House of Robert Maw, an Officer of the Cust
at the Port of Scarborough, situate in Scarborough in
County of York, particularly on the Night of Satu
the 13th ultimo, when the Rioters broke his Wind
and made every possible effort to gain an entrance
his Dwelling-house, with intent to do him and his Fa
some bodily Harm:
The said Commissioners are hereby pleased, in o
to bring to justice the Persons who have been guil
the said Outrage, to offer a Reward of
ONE HUNDRED POUNDS
To any Person or Persons who shall discover or cau
be discovered any one or more of the Persons act
concerned therein, to be paid on Conviction, by the
lector of His Majesty's Customs, at the Port of Scarbor
By Order of the Commissioners,
G. DELAVAUD, S

CUSTOM HOUSE LONDON,
10th March, 1823.

WHEREAS it has been represented to the Com
sioners of His Majesty's Customs, that a vi
Outrage was committed on the Person of WILLIAM I
son, of Scarborough, in the County of York, Farmer
the 15th ultimo, near High Peasholm, by a numbe
Persons riotously assembled about him, some of w
seized him by the Collar, threw Dirt and Stones at
kicked him over his body, legs, and thighs in a most i
man, manner, and then dragged him into Tanner S
in Scarborough, where they threw large Stones at
which knocked him down, and by which, his Head, N
and right Eye were dreadfully injured, and the said V
LIAM DAWSON was placed in the most imminent dang
his life:
The said Commissioners are hereby pleased, in ord
bring to justice the Persons who have been guilty of
said Outrage, to offer a Reward of
ONE HUNDRED POUNDS
To any Person or Persons who shall discover or caus
be discovered any one or more of the Persons who a
actually concerned therein, to be paid upon Convict
by the Collector of His Majesty's Customs, at the I
of Scarborough.
By Order of the Commissioners,
G. DELAVAUD, Se

York, a broadsheet entitled 'On the late Barbarous Murder of Mr James Law by William Mead, the Government Hireling Murderer' was fixed to Whitby bridge and distributed throughout the district. Even before Law's death, a press handout had been prepared, which was then printed in the *York Courant,* the *Sheffield Independent,* the *York Herald, Leeds Independent, Hull Advertiser,* and the *Doncaster Gazette.*

The statement gave a long and very partisan view of events, and employed a flowery, melodramatic style of prose to paint a biased picture of premeditated murder. According to the statement, Mead formed 'diabolical intention' of taking Law's life as he returned from market. This 'atrocious resolve' was to 'satiate his horrid thirst for blood'. It alleged that Mr Law purposely delayed his journey until the early hours of the morning, 'judging by that time, the eye of malice would be closed', but 'William Mead, like a staunch murderer' had waited for his victim 'through the lonesome stillness of the night' and 'discharged the murderous ball'.

It was thought by many from the language and style of reporting that the author was Page, the solicitor acting for the prosecution against Mead.

The trial of Mead and Belt for the murder of James Law was scheduled to be heard at the same Yorkshire Lent Assizes as that which Scott was found guilty of the burglary at John Dodsworth's Harwood Dale farm. The latter case had been heard against the background of Law's death and the subsequent disturbances, which perhaps helps to explain a verdict that the presiding Judge clearly felt was against the weight of evidence. It did not augur well for William Mead and Robert Belt.

It is perhaps not surprising under these circumstances, that the defence counsel did their utmost to delay the trial. On the opening day, 18 March, they protested to the Judge that George Brown, who was seen as a key witness by both sides, was being prevented from attending. His father had sworn an affidavit that the boy was being held against his will in a house at York. When he had gone to collect his son, several people had seized the boy and forcibly detained him. There had been a disturbance in the street involving the solicitor Page, Haxby, the Burniston constable, and two people who had been witnesses against Scott and Bailey. The defence asked for and obtained a writ of *habeas corpus* to produce George Brown at the trial, which was then delayed until 25 March 1823.

When the trial next began, Mr Williams for the defendants rose to demand that the trial be postponed yet again because 'systematic attempts had been made to poison the public mind and to prejudice the opinions of the jury'. He read out the article from the newspapers (mentioned previously), the verses about Mead's perjury and the broadsheet, 'laying the greatest emphasis possible on the most objectionable words'. He further produced a sworn affidavit that prosecution witnesses arriving in York in two post-chaises, had scattered copies of the verses as they had driven through the city street. He 'was reliably informed' that Page was one of the passengers in the chaises. He reminded the Judge that it had been necessary to obtain a writ of *habeas corpus* to ensure that George Brown was free to give evidence. The defence had been hindered in preparing its case because of the deliberate slowness in returning the written depositions of witnesses to the court and the defence solicitor had been prevented from gaining access to Mead's house in Burniston by Haxby the constable. Under these circumstances, he submitted that William Mead and Robert Belt were not likely to receive a fair and impartial trial.

Following William's opening speech the trial was adjourned until the following day, mainly to allow Page time to answer the charge of being involved at that level. In a sworn statement, he stated that he did not know that the broadsheet had been distributed in York and was not privy to such distribution. He had neither authorised, directed or advised it. Both the defence counsel and the Judge noted that Page had confined his denial solely to events in York.

Jones, the prosecuting counsel, objected to the postponement. He argued that the jury was quite capable of ignoring the pamphlets. If people were to be disqualified from serving as jurors because they had read an account of what had happened in a newspaper, no offender 'in these days of education' would be brought to trial. He suspected that the defence was simply trying to delay matters for as long as possible. The prosecution 'had no public purse to meet the costs, in contrast to the defence. By what good fortune the prisoner, who had been a witness for Government, had four counsel, his friend opposite might answer. If these proceedings were to be carried on, the effect would be the prisoners must escape, for no private prosecution could stand such warfare. He hoped the question was not a political one.'

The Judge ruled that witnesses who had chosen to come to York several days earlier than was necessary and who had distributed inflammatory publications in the assize town, could have done so only to improperly influence those people into whose hands they fell. Under all circumstances it was his duty to agree to the trial being postponed until the following assizes.

Having succeeded in their first objective of delaying the trial, the defence lawyers then applied for a writ of *certiorari* to remove the case from the Yorkshire Assizes to the court of the King's Bench in London. The Lord Chief Justice felt the Court was in a considerable difficulty. The publications the defence complained about were a grievous misconduct and one that might well prejudice a fair trial, but if the writ was granted the trial would certainly be delayed and might never take place. The prosecutors might not be able to face the costs of pursuing the case, bringing witnesses to London and maintaining them there. Under the circumstances it was right to refuse the application and the trial must be heard in Yorkshire (Figure 9).

Robert Belt is a somewhat shadowy figure in these events, a peaceable man in his early thirties, who kept a public house. Although he was a friend of Mead, he had played no part in earlier occurrences. He had arranged to spend the night of the shooting at Thomas Brown's house at Burniston and accompany him and his son to Whitby the following day, but, at the last moment, he had slept at Mead's house instead.

William Mead was thirty-six years of age, mild-mannered, 'tradesmanlike' and respectable looking, but with a confident air, even jaunty. He wore a rose in the buttonhole of his coat throughout the trial. He remained very composed, writing short notes to his counsel during the hearing and showing no anxiety when the jury was out. Belt was much more affected by the trial, but both men appeared to be in good spirits when they were brought into court on Monday, 21 July 1823.

The case was still causing considerable excitement and a large

Figure 9. A detail of the York Assizes in the precincts of York Castle. From an engraving in Drake's *History of York*, 1736

crowd assembled before six o'clock in the morning ready to be admitted at seven-thirty. The press interest was such that the Under Sheriff supplied the reporters with tickets and arranged for them to be let into the courtroom early. The gallery windows were removed in an attempt to get more air into the crowded room. It was nine o'clock before Mr Justice Holroyd took his seat, but it took a further hour to empanel the jury. All potential jurors from the East and North Ridings were excluded and sixty-six names were called before there was satisfaction. Finally at about ten o'clock Mr Jones rose for the prosecution to ask the jury 'not to make the case a political issue', but the pressure and disorder in the public galleries was such that it was several minutes before he could be heard.

Inevitably a greater part of the morning was spent outlining the events of James Law's return from Scarborough. Dodsworth, Watson and Hineson gave their version of the shooting and medical evidence was called about the nature of the wound and the cause of death. Witnesses testified to hearing the sound of breaking glass from Mead's window before the shot was fired and Jones showed that when the window was examined the glass had been broken from the inside. In one sense however, much of this evidence was secondary to the main question, for Mead neither denied breaking the window nor discharging the shot. The vital issue in the trial was whether he was justified in doing so. If his actions were not justified then the fact that he had fired the shot would not help the unfortunate Belt, for in law, if Belt had aided and abetted Mead, the question of who had actually pulled the trigger was immaterial. The act of one was the act of both and Robert Belt would be equally guilty of murder.

The defence was able to achieve a significant success in the cross-examination of John Watson. Despite an objection from the prosecution, the Judge ruled that Watson could be questioned about events in Scarborough on the day Law was shot. The defence was thus able to bring out details of the mob attack on John Dobson and, significantly, that Ann Dawson had told Mead what had happened in town. This was to prove the central issue of the trial. If Mead could show that he was genuinely apprehensive for his safety, then his actions could be defended and if he could show that his house was actually under attack, then the firing of the gun might even be justified. The way in which the defence was able to establish that Mead knew the way the smugglers had treated Dobson in Scarborough earlier that day was a strong point in his defence.

In this context, the causeway outside Mead's house was crucial to his defence. The jury were shown an accurate model of the scene made by the defence. It showed the raised causeway in front of the house measuring some two to three feet wide and three feet from the road surface, but broken in places, where, it was argued by the defence, horses could be ridden up to the house itself. If the smugglers had simply sat on their horses in the middle of the street below Mead's window, taunting him by their singing and insults, such behaviour might be annoying, even frightening, but would fall short of justifying his use of the pistol. If, on the other hand, they were actually on the causeway, banging on the door and windows in a manner which suggested that they were trying to force an entry, then Mead might successfully plead self-defence. Both sides were well aware of the importance of this issue and all the smugglers were closely cross-examined on the point, with the other witnesses removed from the courtroom. All denied alighting from their horses and were adamant that they had not ridden on to the causeway, nor hammered on the windows.

There were independent witnesses. The prosecution called Elizabeth Jennison, who had lain in bed with her mother listening to events. She was immediately next door to Mead, separated only by a thin partition, but without the benefit of a window overlooking the road. She heard Law's party, but there had been no attack on the house, no trampling on the causeway and no knocking on Mead's door and window. The defence tried to discredit her by showing that she was on bad terms with Mead's wife. She had been forced to leave the Methodist Church three years before because of an adulterous relationship with a married man. Mead's wife had 'made free with me with her tongue. She talked scandal about a man and me.' They also produced a witness who claimed to have overheard Elizabeth Jennison persuading Mead's young daughter, Dorothy, that she had not heard anything threatening on the night and that she would go to gaol if she said that she had. According to this witness, the eleven-year-old child had replied, 'Oh Betty, you must have heard the horses upon the causeway and did you not hear the knocking at the door?'

Neither Elizabeth Jennison for the prosecution, nor Mary Halliday, the defence witness called to undermine her story, were convincing witnesses and all really depended upon the evidence of George Brown. Described as 'a young boy' he was without obvious links to either party. George was the youth who had been held by the prosecution in York without his father's knowledge, in an apparent attempt to prevent him from giving evidence.

George Brown lived at Burniston with his father, close to the house of William Mead. On the night in question he had been up and about at two o'clock in the morning. He was excited and could not sleep because he was to set out at dawn with his father and Robert Belt to visit his sister at Lofthouse, beyond Whitby. Robert Belt had been expected to be sleeping in the Brown household and had stayed instead with Mead only at the last moment. The boy testified that soon after getting up and lighting a fire, he heard 'a noise like knocking at doors or windows'. He thought it was from Billy Mead's house, because 'they' (the smugglers) had been there a night or two before when it was the talk of the town that they had been breaking in the window shutters. He had opened the door of his house to look out. 'When I was at the door, I heard the noise as if of knocking. I thought it came from William Mead's door; after the second knocking, I heard the report of a gun or pistol instantly.' After the shooting Belt had come round and joined his father and they had all set out for Lofthouse as planned.

The prosecution case took up the whole of the first day until 6.30pm, when the Judge adjourned proceedings and placed the jury under the custody of a court bailiff for the night. They shared the Grand Jury Room where beds and refreshments were provided by the High Sheriff. The jury returned to the court at eight o'clock next morning, but it was not until nine o'clock that the Judge took his seat. The defence opened their case.

An important witness was John Dobson, who was taken through his experiences in Scarborough on the afternoon of Law's death. The defence established that Mead was fully aware of the way he had been treated by Law and Dodsworth. They called Ann Dawson to testify that she had informed Mead of the events in Scarborough on the same day that they occurred. She was also able to confirm that George Brown had told her of the banging on William Mead's door when she had seen him at five o'clock in the morning at Staintondale, as the Browns and Robert Belt had rested on their way to Lofthouse. She admitted that because of her evidence she was now too frightened to return to Scarborough.

Mr Justice Holroyd's summing-up lasted for nearly four hours. The key passages concentrated on the law of trespass. Civil trespass did not justify the firing of the pistol. If the jury was satisfied that James Law and his party had done nothing more than ride up to the house of Mead and sing songs, then no matter how offensive and irritating their actions were, that did not justify the assault on them. If there had been no attack on the house, no violence offered and there was no reasonable apprehension to expect an attack, then the death of Law was murder. However, a man's dwelling-house was his castle, his place of refuge. If this was invaded in the middle of the night, it was almost like an assault upon the person. If William Mead had reasonable grounds for believing that he and his family were in personal danger, then his actions might amount to manslaughter or might even be fully justified.

The jury took just twenty-five minutes to find William Mead guilty of manslaughter and to find Robert Belt not guilty. The Judge called it 'a most proper verdict on the evidence' and accepted that Law and the others had behaved 'in a very improper and outrageous manner'. Mead though, had shown that he did not have 'sufficient regard for the life of a fellow creature'. The Judge in his sentence however was inclined to leniency because Mead had already spent some considerable time in prison and must have suffered greatly because of what had happened on that night. His final verdict was that William Mead should spend two years in prison. The *York Courant* delayed publication that day in order to carry the account of the trial and verdict.

The case despite its conclusion continued to arouse political passions. The Tory newspaper in York, which had campaigned for William Mead's acquittal, was exultant that the murder charge had failed and attacked the Whig inclined *York Courant* for printing the first prejudiced account of Law's death. This, it argued, had aroused such animosity against Mead that it had been difficult to hold a fair trial. The *York Courant* defended its actions, complaining about a tirade of abuse in the Tory journal and talked darkly of preferring to see ten guilty men go free rather than one innocent man suffer. The guilty, it concluded, would one day face a higher Judge.

Other men however had still to face an earthly court. Numerous people had been arrested after the disorders in Scarborough and Burniston. Some like Watson and Scott were prominent smugglers, others were simply caught up in events and now faced trial for riot and assault. Others like Ben Topham had fled before they could be seized.

The first of these trials concerned the riots in Scarborough and the assault on John Dawson. After hearing the prosecution evidence, the Judge interrupted the defence counsel. 'I will tell you what my opinion is; that there was a violent ferment in the town of Scarborough and that in the midst of such ferment, persons acted under wrong feelings.' He gave a clear hint that if the defendants accepted the charges they would be dealt with leniently. The prosecution indicated that they would accept the defendants' own bond to keep the peace. On this basis, the remaining cases were dealt with quickly, but in one instance, passions still ran deep and were still sufficiently inflamed for the defendants to refuse to be bound over. The Crown decided not to proceed and the trial was stopped. In this decision it was seen that there was perhaps a general desire to see calm and peace restored to the town. This may have been an optimistic ideal, for before the defendants were dismissed, Mr Page, as always the solicitor for the smuggling fraternity, rose to complain that the Crown witnesses had begun to insult those on the other side. It was more than likely that it would be some considerable time before the rival factions left Scarborough at peace.

In conclusion, an incident in the year 1817, three years before the smugglers landed their illicit cargo at Salt Pans, sheds an interesting light on William Mead's character. At that date although he was described as a considerable farmer at Stainton, he was in embarrassing circumstances. A writ was issued against him, presumably for debt, and in the normal way, the Sheriff issued a warrant for his arrest. The officer entrusted with carrying out the duty discovered that Mead was at his brother's house. It was also thought that Mead would resist arrest and so the officer set five men in hiding around the house to try and catch him in the open. He then took himself off to a nearby public house to await developments.

After lying in ambush for some time, the sheriff's officers saw the door cautiously open, William Mead look around then start to cross

Figure 10. 'Smugglers attacked'. A popular and romanticised nineteenth century print by an unknown artist showing revenue men capturing smugglers.

the yard. As they moved to arrest him, unfortunately they were seen and Mead dashed back to the house but was grabbed in the act of trying to close the door (Figure 10). One of the five officers, Joseph Trott, put his knee between the door and frame to prevent it fully closing. Mead, half-held through the gap, called for his brother to bring an axe and struck several blows with the cutting edge to Trott's knee, wounding him severely. The door was finally forced opened and both brothers arrested. They were charged with grievous bodily harm.

At the subsequent trial, their counsel, Mr Gilby, put up in their defence three legal objections to the prosecution case. Firstly, they had produced in court the warrant authorising the sheriff's officers to take Mead into custody, but failed to produce the writ on which the warrant was based. The Judge agreed that this should have been in court. Secondly, since the district of Pickering-cum-Lythe was a separate jurisdiction, the writ could not be executed at that place by the Sheriff's officers. A mandate should have been directed to the Chief Bailiff of the district commanding him to execute the warrant. Finally, Gilby's third argument was that the actions of the five assistants was illegal. They were not acting in the presence of the Sheriff's officer and aiding him in the execution of his duty as the officer was elsewhere in the public house.

The Judge agreed. There were too many legal objections for the case to proceed and he directed the jury to acquit the two brothers.[4]

In 1828 Mead approached various persons in the Leeds area claiming to be seeking the rightful heirs to inheritances unclaimed in Chancery. The *Leeds Intelligencer* reported that the number of Leeds people who were willing to hand over copies of wills, registers of baptisms and money to cover Mead's expenses 'exceeds belief'. Needless to say, William Mead then disappeared, but his obituary, sent through the post, appeared soon afterwards in a London newspaper. It was later reported that Mead had been seen in the towns of Goole and Hull.[5] By the year 1830 however, he was back in the Scarborough area.

In an interesting twist to his life, following his last criminal act in 1830, William Mead found himself once more in the dock at York Assizes in July of that year, charged with stealing two oxen and a heifer from a farmer named Stubbs who lived at Harwood Dale. The animals had been left grazing in a field two miles from the farm buildings, but had been removed by Mead during the night. At four-thirty in the morning he was observed driving them through Saltersgate 'by a man named Belt, who is ostler at an inn there'.

Figure 11. The condemned cell in York Prison in which William Mead would have languished before his execution.

Robert Belt, onetime friend of Mead, was to be the prime prosecution witness at York – an irony. Mead had then continued on to Malton, where he had employed a man to drive the beasts to York, whilst he followed in comfort by carrier's wagon. The aggrieved owner had finally caught up with Mead at the *Wagon and Horses* near Walmgate Bar in York. The missing animals were found in the landlord's field nearby.

William Mead had nothing to say in his defence at the trial. The jury found him guilty and he was sentenced to death (Figures 11 & 12).[6]

Notes and References

1. *Hull Packet* 3 February 1823.
2. *York Courant* 31 December 1822.
3. Dykes, *Smuggling on the Yorkshire Coast.* Dalesman Publishing Company, 1978, p25.
4. *Hull Packet* 12 August 1817.
5. Dykes, p26.
6. *Hull Advertiser* 30 July 1830.

Figure 12. An execution behind York Castle. From Drake's *History of York*

8. CURIOSITIES OF THE YORKSHIRE COAST

by Eileen Rennison

WHAT CONSTITUTES A CURIOSITY? The dictionary defines it as 'anything curious, rare or unusual, odd or strange'. The Yorkshire coast by this definition has many curiosities reminding us of a bygone age: unusual buildings, follies, odd memorials and inscriptions, and strange objects with curious or historical associations. Many are familiar features in the landscape, and indeed, some may be so familiar that no one any longer stops to wonder what they are, what they were used for, or how they came to be there.

If one were to stretch a point and consider the Yorkshire coast to be, as it once was, reaching from the Tees to the Humber, it would be impossible in writing about coastal curiosities to omit mention of the oldest lifeboat in the world, the *Zetland*, which is housed in the tiny museum at Redcar. Built in 1800 by Henry Greathead to a modified design by William Wouldhave, both of South Shields, it served for seventy-eight years and saved 500 lives. However, like the allegedly smallest church in the country at Upleatham, it is now laid claim to by Cleveland.

Old customs whose original purpose no longer exist are often still continued, and at Staithes one can still see the occasional old dame wearing a traditional Staithes bonnet, though it may be for the benefit of the visitors. In the nineteenth century they featured in the photographs of Frank Meadow Sutcliffe the Whitby photographer, in their authentic setting. Today tourists may even buy one for use as a sun hat. They serve this purpose well but their true use, though open to speculation, was certainly of a practical and workaday nature. Made up of nine pieces cut from a yard of cotton cloth, the bonnet has a double crown, a double pleated frill almost three inches wide at the front and ties with a bow at the back. The women of Staithes worked beside their menfolk and carried the bait and fishing lines on their heads down to the boats. The bonnets would serve to protect the head and hair and also keep the hair free from fishy smells. When it was common to wear bonnets, the Staithes bonnet was peculiar to the village and remains a curious relic of the past.

A short way further down the coast, between Staithes and Runswick Bay is the tiny abandoned harbour of Port Mulgrave.

Many visitors to the coast hereabouts are unaware of this little 'lost port' with its beautiful cliff-top views and historical interest. It was constructed in the nineteenth century at the height of the ironstone boom, by Charles Palmer, of Jarrow, who had furnaces there to extract the iron ore. He was also the founder of the Grinkle Park Mining Company, and had the idea of moving iron ore from the mine to the port and then shipping it from there to his works at Jarrow and consequently reducing costs. A narrow gauge railway transported the ore from the mine with a stationary engine pulling the trucks through a mile-long tunnel and then lowering them down the steep cliffs. The entrance to this tunnel although bricked up, can still be seen.

The mine was finally closed in the 1920s due to the importation of cheaper iron ore from abroad, and Port Mulgrave which at its peak shipped 3,000 tons of ore per week, was abandoned, a victim of progress, but it remains as a reminder of the once proud industrial heritage of this coast.

Many of the smaller curiosities are to be found in churches – always a rich source of interesting relics and folklore. St Oswald's church, magnificently sited high above the steep Lythe bank, underwent restoration in 1910 (Figure 1) when several stone

Figure 1. St Oswalds church, Lythe after restoration. *Photograph by Tom Watson from the collection of Alan Whitworth*

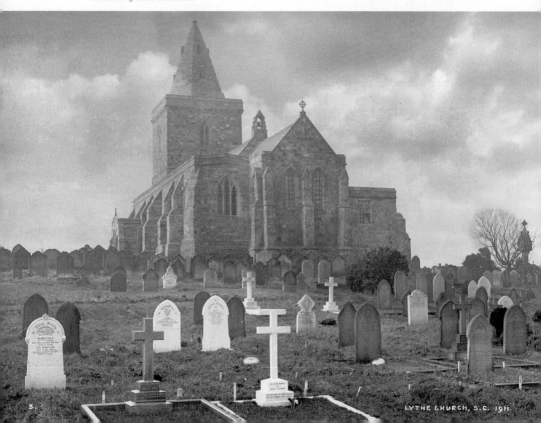

fragments of Anglo-Danish sculpture were discovered, built into the walls of the old church. These came from a Viking graveyard, the last resting-place of settlers who landed near Lythe in the year 867. One of these interesting carved stones, now inside the church, shows figures apparently engaged in the sport of wrestling. But perhaps stranger still are the two ancient musical instruments, known as ophicleides, which hand either side of a doorway in the church (Figure 2). Large and black in colour, these rare and now obsolete bass wind instruments were developed from the early instrument called a serpent, mentioned frequently in the Bible, and were once used here at Lythe to support the singing in the choir.

Just a few miles from Lythe, is Whitby, which must surely contain more curiosities than any other place on the Yorkshire coast. Perhaps too many to mention, but we cannot pass by without alluding to at least one, perhaps the strangest of them all.

In the town museum situated in Pannet Park, is a reminder of an occupation that although hazardous, was not at all honourable, and of the superstitious means that the men who went about this occupation employed to safeguard themselves. The 'Hand of Glory' is a grisly relic of criminal history; a human hand cut from the body of a criminal hanging on the gallows which burglars took on their nefarious activities in the belief it would protect them from being caught – and perhaps, more strangely, even make them invisible and their victims remain asleep.

To complete the charm, the dried and shrivelled hand was used as a candle-holder, the candle itself being made from fat from the body of a hanged man and the wick from his hair. As the gruesome result was placed in the hand and lit, special ritual chants were uttered over it to call up the magic. Once lit, the magic could only be undone if the candle were extinguished with milk or blood!

The 'Hand of Glory' in the Whitby Museum is thought to have last been used in 1820, and the last recorded use of one was in 1831. As burglary was punishable by death until the year 1837, burglars were perhaps naturally more than usually anxious not to be

Figure 2. The ophicleides in St Oswald's church, Lythe.

caught. It is thought that when the penalty for burglary was reduced from death to imprisonment the sting was taken out of the crime and the employment of the 'Hand of Glory' gradually fell into disuse.

One last curiosity of Whitby, a natural phenomenon due to the northern orientation of the town, is the odd fact that during the two week period before and after the Summer Solstice on 21 June, the sun can be seen both rising and setting over the sea. When a writer first pointed this out in the nineteenth century, such a statement was greeted by derision from the reading public.

On the corner of the A169 road from Whitby to Sleights at its junction with the A171 stands a squat stone pillar marking the spot where the first enemy aeroplane to be shot down in the Second World War crashed into a group of trees beside the nearby farmhouse on 3 February 1940. Group Captain Peter Townsend, who later became famous for his romance with Princess Margaret, had engaged the German Heinkel bomber in his Hurricane fighter two miles out to sea and pursued it inland. The German rear-gunner Karl Missy, despite being severely wounded returned his fire continuously as they flew over the town. After the German Heinkel crashed he was taken to Whitby Cottage Hospital where one of his legs had to be amputated. Peter Townsend out of respect for his bravery paid him a visit there.

Figure 3. The eighteenth century folly in Littlebeck Wood known as The Hermitage. *Drawing by P B Rennison.*

Between the road junction where the pillar is situated, which is one of a pair taken from the bridge in the valley below that was washed away in a flood in 1935 which was later replaced by the present high-rise bridge over the River Esk, is a narrow stone-paved way with the mysterious and intriguing name of *Featherbed Lane*. It is only about four feet wide and has been described as the 'narrowest highway in England', qualifying as a highway rather than pathway because of its paved nature. It is in fact an old stone 'trod' wide enough for the passage of a pack horse, and providing a dry route for the carriage of goods between villages since the days of King James I.

Beyond Sleights, in the small valley of Littlebeck, not far from the splendid waterfall of *Falling Foss*, in Littlebeck Woods is a curious cell known as 'the Hermitage' (Figure 3). It is hollowed out from a single huge boulder and the initials 'GC' and the date 1790 are carved above the pointed doorway. The initials are those of George Chubb, a local schoolmaster, who engaged a sailor named Jeffrey to do the work as part of a scheme to enhance the grounds of *Newton House* for its owner Jonas Brown. Follies of all kinds were the height of fashion in the eighteenth and early nineteenth century, and it was considered extremely 'smart' for a gentleman to install a hermit, living without the barest comforts of life, in a cell on his estate.

Fylingthorpe, near Robin Hoods Bay can boast possibly the strangest but most attractive pig-sty in the country (Figure 4). It was erected in 1883 by the eccentric Squire John Walter Barry of *Fyling*

Figure 4. The ornate pig-sty at Fylingthorpe, near Robin Hoods Bay. *Drawing by P B Rennison.*

Hall, who travelled abroad a great deal and brought back unusual plants and trees as well as architectural ideas. The building housing the pigs in such magnificent style is like a Greek temple, decorated in ochre, gold and red colours and has a grand portico and pediment supported on Ionic columns. It took three men two years to build, however the delay was mostly because Squire Barry kept changing his mind about the design. Stone used in the construction had to be brought from a nearby quarry by horse-drawn sleds. Today this unusual building with its unlikely origin is no longer home to swine, apart from one stone statue of a pig, instead it has been fully restored in recent years and converted to an unusual holiday home by the Landmark Trust.

Figure 5. An example of a 'Coffin Window' in a cottage at Robin Hoods Bay.

In Robin Hoods Bay the red roofed houses seem to tumble down the cliff to the sea. It is said that many of the old cottages have secret rooms and cupboards, and there are tunnels from house to house; a legacy of the time when it was the centre of smuggling activities. Many of the old dwellings are small with twisting stairs. In several cottages a small window known as a 'coffin window' is placed at the bend of the staircase (Figure 5) just large enough to facilitate the removal of a coffin which could otherwise not be manoeuvred down the winding stairs. This practical solution to a problem results in a curious architectural feature peculiar to this small seaside village.

Further south, Scarborough has the distinction of being England's oldest holiday resort and was a Spa as early as 1626 when its medicinal waters were discovered and exploited (Figure 6). It was also the first resort to encourage sea bathing for the promotion of health.

Figure 6. Detail of the well and water-servers at Scarborough Spa. From Francis Place's drawing of 1715

Figure 7. The Rotunda Museum, Scarborough.

In 1829 the Rotunda Museum (Figure 7) with its unusual circular plan was built by the Scarborough Philosophical Society to house the collection of rocks and fossils of William Smith. By his actions and industry he earned himself the title of 'father of geology' being the first to identify and classify the age of rocks by the fossils in the differing strata. The museum was originally laid out in layers for the easy understanding of his principals, and a unique viewing platform on wheels enabled each layer to be studied as it moved around the circular museum building. This platform can still be seen, though not in use in the museum, which also contains the 'Pancake Bell' of old. This was rung at noon on Shrove Tuesday to warn the housewives that it was time to prepare the pancakes. Pancakes are traditionally thought to be the means of using up the ingredients before the fasting of Lent. Skipping on the Foreshore is another curious custom in Scarborough on Shrove Tuesday, with people coming into the town especially to join in. There are many theories but no firm conclusions for this custom, though skipping was in ancient times said to have magical properties possibly linked to the season of spring and fertility.

About six miles south-west from Scarborough, in the village of Wykeham, the church has an odd but impressive gateway complete with broach spire, buttresses and a clock face. If it looks like the

Figure 8. A drawing of the 'Boy Bishop' memorial, *Wykeham.*

upper part of a fourteenth century church that is not surprising since that is exactly what it was. It is all that remains of the chapel of St Mary and St Helen, now serving as the entrance to the churchyard of All Saints church built in 1853.

Further south on the coast at Filey the church of St Oswald contains a relic of a strange old ceremony from the Middle Ages, that was discontinued after the Reformation as being to sacrilegious. Beside the 'Fishermen's Window' commemorating those men lost at sea and never recovered, is the memorial of a 'Boy Bishop' dating from between 1250 and 1300 (Figure 8). The 'Boy Bishop' was chosen from the scholars of the Parish Grammar School or the church choir and invested with the full regalia of a bishop. Between 6 December, St Nicholas' Day and Holy Innocents' Day on 28 December, he presided over the Church services and was responsible for the boys dressed as priests. From the appearance of the memorial it would appear that the youth commemorated here may perhaps have died in 'office'.

Side by side on the village green at Hunmanby are the lock-up and the pinfold, which may be curiosities to us today but were once commonplace features of rural life. The pinfold was a simple enclosure in which stray animals could be kept until claimed by their owners upon payment of a small fine to the Pinder, the man in charge of the pinfold. The pinfold at Hunmanby is circular in shape but unlike many that still survive today, it was built of cobbled stones gathered from the seashore. The lock-up, dating from 1834, has two small cells with tiny windows and narrow doorways, and was used mainly to hold drunks and disorderly revellers after Feasts and Fairs, or other law breakers until they were sober or handed over to the magistrates for trial. Hunmanby is unusual in having both a lock-up and a pinfold, although at Burniston, on the outskirts of Scarborough, the village has a pinfold and a cock-pit adjacent where fights between cock birds were held.

In a field at Wold Newton a few miles inland a brick obelisk marks the spot where a meteorite fell in 1795. The object which fell to earth measured a yard long and twenty-eight inches across, and was black and glassy smooth. Mr Topham, a magistrate who lived nearby had the meteorite sent to London to be examined by scientists who until then had not believed stories of stones falling from the sky! The meteorite, the first to be acknowledged as such, can still be viewed in the Natural History Museum in London.

At Flamborough two lighthouses stand on Flamborough Head. The chalk tower put up in 1674 by Sir John Clayton is the oldest remaining lighthouse in England (Figure 9). It relied simply on a coal fire in a cresset on top of the tower to provide illumination. Sir John tried to collect tolls from passing ships to pay for it, which proved difficult and which practice was insufficient to maintain it. In time it fell into disuse. However, in 1806 Trinity House recognised the need for a lighthouse here and the present one was erected nearer the sea. It is said that a John Maston, of Bridlington, built it within five months, without the use of scaffolding. The flashing light from the ninety-two feet high tower can be seen twenty-one miles out at sea.

In the church at Flamborough village is a Rood Loft, one of only two surviving in Yorkshire. The word 'rood' means cross and in particular refers to the crucifix on a chancel screen of which many of the latter remain. A

Figure 9. The lighthouse at Flamborough, dated 1674.

large number of churches dating from the fourteenth century until the period of the Reformation had a gallery - the rood loft - above the chancel arch screen, from which part of the church service was conducted. These rood lofts were among the numerous church features destroyed by order of King Henry VIII as he flung off papal allegiance in 1534 and which continued down to the accession of his daughter Elizabeth in 1558.

There are other curiosities to be found in St Oswald's church. A replica of the Royal Pardon granted to Walter Strickland in 1660 by King Charles II despite his long and treasonable association with the King's enemies. And the tomb of Sir Marmaduke Constable portrays the strange legend concerning his death in 1530 caused allegedly by accidentally swallowing a toad in a drink of water. The toad it is said then ate away his heart! His tomb is surmounted by a skeletal ribcage containing his heart and a toad. A very strange memorial and a very strange belief.

In Bridlington Old Town, along Applegarth Lane, a tiny building only twelve feet square is the oldest and smallest Nonconformist

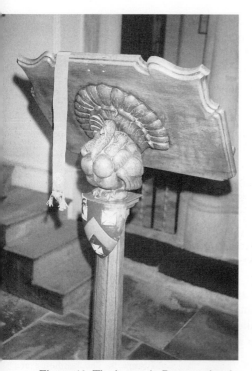

Figure 10. The lectern in Boynton church carved in the shape of a turkey above the arms of Strickland.

Meeting House in East Yorkshire. A minuscule Baptist Chapel built in 1699 that served only twenty members who were the first recorded Baptist congregation in the East Riding established in the previous year. Though it looks like a small brick outhouse, its significance and historical association makes it an interesting monument worthy of protection as a building of architectural importance.

When Queen Henrietta Maria landed at Bridlington in 1643 from Holland, where she had been to raise money to support King Charles, she stayed overnight at nearby *Boynton Hall* a few miles inland, but left next day to join the King taking away all the family silver, paying for it with only a portrait of herself. In the church beside the hall gates the lectern shows not the usual eagle but a turkey (Figure 10). William Strickland, of *Boynton Hall* sailed to the New World with Sebastian Cabot and brought back what was then an unknown bird. The unusual lectern is a reminder of Strickland's introduction of turkey's into this country which bird is also incorporated into the family crest.

In the neighbouring village of Rudston, the largest standing stone in the country is situated among the gravestones in the churchyard in close proximity to the church (Figure 11). It is twenty-six feet high and sixteen feet in circumference at its base, and another twenty-five feet is buried in the ground. The huge gritstone monolith is some four thousand years old and is almost certainly situated in a pagan holy place, adopted, as so many were, by the early Christian Church. A legend associated

Figure 11. The prehistoric monolith in Rudston churchyard, the largest standing stone in the country.

Figure 12. The curious monument, Woodhenge, situated on top of Trusey Hill, between Bridlington and Hornsea.

with the stone is that the devil, angered by the building of the church on a sacred pagan site, threw the stone like a spear to destroy it, but missed the target. Completely untrue of course, it is another example of attributing to the devil what cannot otherwise be explained.

A mile or two from Bridlington, the East Riding has its own Greek temple at Carnaby. It was erected by Sir George Strickland, of *Boynton Hall,* as a folly in the late eighteenth century. Although constructed of brick it took its inspiration from the 'Temple of Winds' in Athens. Octagonal, lofty and topped by a lantern, it gave excellent unhindered views across the countryside. During the Second World War it was used for military purposes. Today the windows are all bricked up but it is still an impressive monument and must have been a wonderful place for family and friends to visit in Sir George's day.

At Barmston, between Bridlington and Hornsea, is one of the most curious memorials on the coast. Nicknamed 'Woodhenge' it was erected by Mr Chris Marshall, a local landowner (Figure 12). It consists of a circle of dead tree trunks preserved and transplanted on the top of *Trusey Hill,* which is reputed to be the site of an ancient monastery. Within and beneath this group lie buried a human skeleton found on the site, a gun carriage from the Great War found on the beach, and a number of other items; the whole forming an eerie memorial to death itself.

In 1844 a Mr Bettison built on his estate a fifty foot high circular tower of decorative brickwork with a crenellated parapet. Modern housing now surrounds this building which had a most unusual purpose. A servant kept watch from it whenever the master was away from home in order to look out for the approach of Mr Bettison's carriage, then word could be passed on to the kitchen so that his meal could be made ready without delay. An interesting glimpse into the social order of the time.

Not far from Bettisons Tower as it has come to be known, stands the church of St Nicholas at Hornsea that has a crypt with a curious history. Unusually it has two rooms and a fireplace, and is said to have once been the home of a witch called Nanny Cankerneedle. At another period it was used by a dishonest verger to store smuggled contraband. During this time the church spire came crashing down onto the building. So shaken was the verger, that he took it as a sign of the wrath of God and had a stroke from which he never recovered.

Withernsea lies south of Hornsea and developed as a seaside resort in Queen Victoria's reign with the coming of the railway. Part of its attraction was a pier almost two thousand feet in length which was eventually destroyed by a ship being driven into it during a storm in October 1880. Today all that remains of this pier is the castellated gateway forming an unusual feature of the modern Promenade.

Also unusual at Withernsea, is the fact that the lighthouse was built among the houses of the main street. When it ceased to serve its original purpose in 1976, it was bought by the sister of the actress Kay Kendal, star of the film *Genevieve* with Kenneth Moore. Their

Figure 13. The fourteenth century tithe barn at Easington, East Yorkshire.

grandfather had been involved in the building of the lighthouse and was the last coxswain of the local lifeboat. The lighthouse now houses a museum of local history and the RNLI, and is a memorial to the actress Kay, who tragically died so young.

At Easington is the only remaining tithe barn in East Yorkshire (Figure 13). Tithes were a payment of one tenth of all the product of the parish for the support of the clergy, and continued in some form from the earliest recorded in AD794 to the nineteenth century. Large barns were needed to store the tithe goods in, which usually consisted of grain. The one at Easington is a typical example, constructed of brick with massive doors and a thatched roof. It dates from the fourteenth century and its size gives an indication of the productivity of the land around that time.

Approaching Kilnsea on the southernmost point of the coast a curious object can be found at some distance across fields. It is a huge device in concrete and shaped like a satellite dish. Little is known about this object, nor when it was first put there, but it is

Figure 14. The Bolinbroke memorial in the garden of *Holyrood House,* Hedon.

believed to be a sound mirror used to locate enemy aeroplanes or zeppelins in the First World War by reflecting and concentrating the sound of their engines. It is approximately four and a half metres wide, four high, and two metres deep at its base. In front of the concave area on a metal post that still survives was attached a microphone. Possibly the strangest relic of the counties coastal defences.

Talk of the coast reminds us of just how much the coast is constantly being eroded. This is indicated here at Kilnsea, by the fact that the *Blue Bell House* when built in 1847 was half a mile from the sea, but by the year 1994 the distance was only 190 yards! This leads us to the final curiosity of the Yorkshire coast that is no longer on its original site due to this coastal erosion.

In 1398 Henry Bolingbroke, son of John of Gaunt, was sent into exile for opposing King Richard II. In 1399 he returned to depose the King and claim the throne, landing at Ravenser, a place now washed away and lost. A column twenty feet high with a heraldic device on the top once marked the spot where Bolingbroke landed. In time it was also lost but was later washed up at Kilnsea in 1818. It was re-erected but inland for safety and now it stands in a quiet garden at *Holyrood House* in Hedon (Figure 14); a reminder not just of Henry Bolingbroke and his abortive attempt to claim the throne of England but also of our lost coastline.

9. Come Rain, Come Shine – The Langtoft Floods

by David Wright

THE LARGE PARISH OF LANGTOFT, irregular in shape, lies on the Wolds about six miles north of Great Driffield and twelve miles due west of Bridlington in the East Riding of Yorkshire (Figure 1). Its situation is high; only in valley bottoms does it include any land lower than two hundred feet above sea-level. Including the depopulated township of Cottam, which lay on the Wolds about one and a half miles south-west of Langtoft village, it extends for about five miles from north-east to south-west across hills and dry valleys. The parish boundaries often run in the valley bottoms. Much of the northern boundary, however, follows *High Street*, on the line of a Roman road,[1] and another part of this boundary seems to have been aligned on a Bronze-Age barrow near Octon cross-roads.[2] A short section of the

Figure 1. Detail of Thomas Jeffreys, map of 1772 showing Langtoft and district.

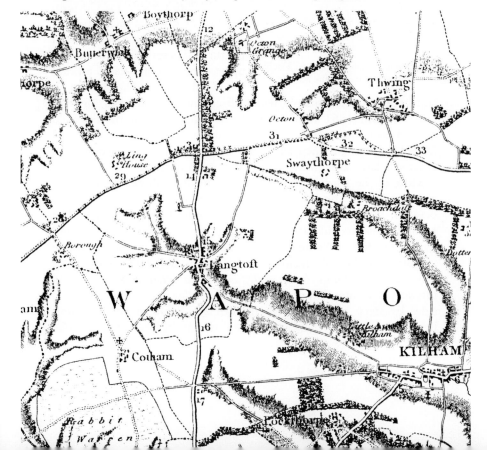

Figure 2. Map of Langtoft village. Kindly supplied by the landlord of the Ship Inn

southern boundary follows a prehistoric earthwork. The total area of the ancient parish was 6,168 acres, of which 2,586 acres lay in Cottam township[3] that was detached from Langtoft in 1935 and combined with Cowlam to form the new civil parish of Cottam.[4]

The landscape of the parish is typical of the high Yorkshire Wolds. The exposed slopes are dissected by many steep-sided dry valleys, the most prominent being that in which Langtoft village lies and which may be the 'long piece of ground' of the place-name.[5] Other place-names include *Tog Dale, Crake Dale, West Dale,* and *Crooked Dale* in Langtoft, and *Bortree Dale, Lambert Dale, Cottam Well Dale,* and *Phillips' Slack* in Cottam. *Lambert Dale* is first mentioned, as 'Lambcotedale', in the twelfth century.[6] There is little woodland apart from shelter-belts around the Wolds farms. The pattern of large regular fields mainly results from the inclosures of 1805 in Langtoft and 1851 in Cottam, before which much of the Wold ground lay in the open fields. Most of the parish is now under arable farming, although since about 1939 an airfield, now disused, has covered a large area in the centre of Cottam township.[7]

Most of the land in the parish is more than three hundred feet above sea-level. The valley in which Langtoft village lies is mainly at between two hundred feet and two hundred and fifty feet. The ground rises steadily from the village to over five hundred and twenty-five feet at the northern end and over five hundred feet at the western boundary. To the north-east it rises to over four hundred and fifty feet before falling again in *Tog Dale* to under three hundred and fifty feet. The situation of the village in a valley surrounded on three sides by steep hills has made it especially liable to flooding after heavy rain. Cottam village lay on the slopes at the head of *Cottam Well*

Dale at between four hundred and twenty-five feet and four hundred and seventy-five feet. To the south a broad belt of land, much of it now covered by the old airfield, lies at over four hundred and seventy-five feet above sea-level. The ground then falls away to under one hundred and fifty feet at the southern boundary.

Langtoft village (Figure 2) lies mainly along the B1249 Driffield-Foxholes road, which is known as *Tire Ewe Hill* south of the village, *Main Street* within it and *Scarborough Gate* to the north (Figure 3). Minor roads converging on the village include Cottam Lane and the Kilham Road, the so-called *Occupation Road* existed by 1772 and formerly led north-westwards to *High Street*. Finally a road known as *West Gate* within the village and *Malton Gate* beyond runs westwards and until at least 1772 led to West Lutton.[8] It now leads only as far as the Weaverthorpe-Cottam road beyond the parish boundary. A fifth road formerly led into the village from Butterwick. Between 1772 and 1817 it was joined to *Scarborough Gate* about a mile north of the village by a short connecting road, now known as *Mill Lane*, and its southern section was blocked.[9] A field road now marks part of its former course. In the early years of the nineteenth century much money was spent on keeping the roads open in winter and on repairing their surfaces.

Nestling as it does, in a bowl, the village of Langtoft has suffered frequent floods over the centuries. Of the three major inundations, the earliest recorded one is that which occurred in 1657, which occurred not many years after Langtoft had been 'very sore infected' with the plague in 1638.[10] This seventeenth century flood, was commemorated by a stone in the wall of a cottage in the village belonging to a Mr. Stork that was exposed, coincidentally, by the later flood of 1892, and indicated that the height of both the former and the latter floodwaters at their raging deepest, had been in the region of eight feet.

Figure 3. Langtoft village.

GreatFlood AT LANGTOTT the 10 DAY CF4 month 1657

Figure 4. A rubbing of the commemorative plaque placed eight feet from the ground recording the 1657 flood.

The village had always been subject to inundation, not only from persistent extreme weather conditions, but also on occasions, after deluges whose ferocity would pose no problem for more favourably situated wold villages sited within the landscape of the rolling East Yorkshire terrain. During past centuries a sudden thunder shower or spring snow thaw would be sufficient to cause a heavy rush of water into the village of Langtoft.

A brief memorial (Figure 4) to the past deluge was once contained within the walls of a cottage and carried the wording, 'Great Flood at Langtoft. The 10th day of the 4th Month. 1657' and was the only recorded evidence of the great disaster visited upon the environs two and a half centuries previous to that of 1892. Evidence of the building materials and methods of construction of earlier times revealed by the demolishing effects of the late-nineteenth century flood waters showed only too clearly the vulnerability to storms and other natural disasters of the rudimentary dwellings of agricultural workers of previous eras.

In May 1853 a terrific thunderstorm broke over Langtoft. There was no accompanying flood, but much damage was wreaked upon the region by forked lightning. Around the vicinity of *Round Hill* to the west of the village, two men were ploughing when lightning struck and killed their horses, whilst simultaneously destroying their ploughs. The men, however, escaped serious injury, suffering only shock and minor scorching to their persons.

The next two decades were uneventful, until a storm on 9 December 1874, completely demolished the partly-built Wesleyan Chapel under construction at that time. The Reverend Jordan Sharp, the Methodist Minister at Langtoft then, recorded the day's events and aftermath in his *Journal*.

On the ninth instant, about 2 o'clock am, our partly-built New Chapel was blown down – excepting the front which appears to stand alright. The windows next [to] Chapel Lane have been partly arched, the front was not in such a forward state, only about two courses of bricks had been laid about the beam above the door. The weather was most changeable, strong frosts and heavy rains, hence the giving way of the building to a violent gale of winds blowing on the morning in question. The weather has since been, and still is, very severe, but hope in God's good providence we shall have in [the] *course of time some fine weather for the rebuilding of the House of God, and when complete may many souls be born there for God.*

The next serious inundation came in 1888. The first villagers to notice the approaching storm reported that it resembled in shape Sir Tatton Sykes's memorial at nearby Sledmere, floating in cloud-form, and approaching from an easterly direction. It too, like the storm of 1853, connected with the contours of the wolds at *Round Hill,* inundating Langtoft from a westerly direction. Fortunately, on this occasion there was no loss of life, animal or human. The Reverend JD Speck, vicar of the parish, tasted the water, declaring it to be 'brackish' and of a salty nature, having been conveyed sixteen miles from the bay at Bridlington. Much damage, however, was done to farmland by the raging torrent. The Savile, Wilson, Featherstone, and Shipley farms suffering the worst damage to crops and hedgerows.

The effect of the deluge on the village was immediate. A vast flowing stream of floodwater forty feet wide sped down *Briggate* to the Cottam-Langtoft road. Lower areas of the township were totally swamped. The inhabitants, caught by surprise, were panic-stricken in the face of the advancing waters. Mothers with children took refuge in the upper rooms of their cottages as the influx of water rapidly attained a depth of four feet in the lower rooms. The duration of the inundation was approximately two hours, within which time doors had burst open and pots, pans, chairs, stools, mats, and other household effects had been carried off by the floodwaters. In one cottage a family of children called for help from the bedroom window as their mother consoled them as best she could from the upper window of a neighbour's home. A cat was seen to be swimming in ever-decreasing circles in a village street totally bemused by events. All of the village pigs were successfully rescued from their sties; but the fate of garden produce had no such fortunate ending. Everything was either ruined or swept away. After the floodwaters had subsided, great stones and large amounts of gravel were found in the village streets. Surrounding fields had been completely stripped of their topsoil by the flooding.

The family home of William and Rachel Wright, my great grandparents, was one of twelve terraced cottages situated on *Westgate* in which cramped circumstances the parents, all of their ten children, with the exception of two eldest sons, and the substantial brood of illegitimate grandchildren existed as best they could. Added to the problems of overcrowding, the cottage in the year 1888, twelve-months after the death of William, suffered much damage following the flood. The Wright family lost all of their possessions, and the cottage, with the other eleven became uninhabitable for a period.

Only four years elapsed before the next and greatest flood visited depredations upon the village. By the mid-afternoon of Sunday 3 July 1892 the people of Langtoft had already begun to sense a feeling of impending doom. It had been the hottest day in living memory. Since lunchtime a great black storm-cloud had been forming beyond the wolds at Cottam and Cowlam. The villagers remembered, all too vividly, the great storm and flood of 1888 when many of them had lost possessions and property. In the early evening many of the inhabitants attended service at St. Peter's Church on the hillside above the village, blissfully ignorant that this place of worship would soon become a sanctuary from the raging storm soon to visit the village below.

At around seven o'clock a Mr Digby Caley, of Malton, was making his way from Cottam to Luttons in a shallow gig when he noticed a vast storm-cloud in the west rapidly approaching Cottam. The atmosphere was oppressively hot, and the early July evening was transformed to black of night. Immense hailstones began to fall, followed by torrential rain, swiftly filling the gig. Mr Caley pulled the horse to a halt, deciding to sit out the storm that had already flooded the road. Through the driving rain he watched a funnel of black cloud reaching down from the skies to *Round Hill*, a mile or so west of Langtoft. Even from the distance of two miles he noticed a great displacement of chalk from the hillside, produced by the waters in the form of a water spout issuing from the storm-cloud.[11] The accompanying electrical storm was the most terrifying spectacle anyone had ever witnessed on the Wolds.

The storm waters, rushing down the hillside, soon filled the valley of *Briggate* and joining forces with another column of water coursing down *Honey Hill* from Cottam, flowed rapidly towards the unsuspecting village of Langtoft nestling in the lower valley. Raging in a torrent thirty yards wide, the floodwaters entered the village at *Westgate* (now called *New Maltongate*) where a row of twelve chalk cottages were instantly inundated. A Mrs Gray, a widow, eighty-five years of age, was the first to be made aware of the deluge. Slamming her front door on the approaching river of water, she ran, as best she could, to the rear of her property in order to climb the stairs to the safety of the upper floor. The floodwaters reached the stairway door just as she attempted to close it behind her, and unfortunately trapped her long black Sabbath dress in the doorway. With water up to her waist and rising, her trapped dress now wedged firmly in the doorway clung tightly, however, she managed with difficulty to discard her outer garments and escape to the bedroom above from which she was eventually rescued.

The river of water, now coursing at a depth of seven feet, carrying with it uprooted crops, trees, and hedgerow material, and further enhanced with furniture, pots, pans, ruined clothing, and all manner of cottagers' possessions, next reached the village pond, flooding the cottages behind. One old village character, believing his salvation lay not in the church on the hillside, but in his ability to contemplate the meaning of life whilst leaning on the top bar of the gate to his property adjacent to the Nook, was immediately put to nature's trial-by-ordeal by the approaching floodwater. He managed with arthritic and octogenarian difficulty to climb the gate and hang on to the guttering of an adjoining building while the waters rose to his knees, until finally rescued, with no obligation of thanks whatsoever to the powers of providence, only a satisfaction at the agility of his mental and physical prowess.

The floodwaters next inundated the joinery shop of Mr Woodmansey situated in *Back Street,* completely demolishing the workshop and washing away all his tools. A Mr Stork and his family, trapped in the bedroom of their home, could only watch as the cottage slowly disintegrated around them. A ladder was lowered onto the roof of their abode from a cottage situated on higher ground to the rear of their property, and they made a precarious escape by this means.

By now the raging torrent also carried a cargo of dismembered haystacks, poultry, dead pigs, a rapidly weakening horse (which did eventually swim to safety), the village pump with chain and two buckets, a threshing machine, Mr Lawty's twenty-one hives of bees, and the walls and palisades that had formerly surrounded the Wesleyan Chapel, along with other sundry building and household debris.

Mr Aquila Sharp, the village carrier, was for a time, extremely concerned about the whereabouts of his children who had been out walking in the direction of the then approaching flood. He was relieved to learn that they had returned in time, and had taken refuge in a neighbour's house.

Figure 5. Mary Wharram (1864-1924) trapped in her Back Street cottage by the flood of 1892.

Figure 6. Florence Wharram (1881-1963), daughter of Richard and Mary Wharram (Fig. 5), trapped with her mother in the flood.

Figure 7. Thomas Wright (1868-1932), whose cottage on New Row, was inundated by the flood of July 1892.

The rescuers of the wife of Richard Wharram, Mary (Figure 5) trapped alone in the family cottage with her baby Florence (Figure 6), and completely surrounded by the rising tide of water, approached the cottage by way of a high narrow wall, saving her and her infant by breaking through the roof of the cottage.

Mr and Mrs Bell, the former a Langtoft schoolmaster, having been away from the village for the weekend, later returned to find their home still flooded to a depth of five feet, with all Mr Bell's valuable collection of books washed away by the flood.

Many of the cottages and other dwellings along *Westgate*, the *Nook*, *Front Street* and *Back Street* were either demolished or partially destroyed including that of Thomas Wright (Figure 7). In total sixty-five houses and cottages had been extensively damaged. Numerous others became at the very least, temporarily uninhabitable due to the lake of muddy silt deposited in the wake of the floodwaters, that lay three feet deep in the lower parts of the village. Also by chemical manure washed down from the surrounding fields, that ruined the clothing, furnishings and other household effects. Fortunately, and almost miraculously, nobody had been killed, but there was much hardship to follow.

The raging torrent, having devastated Langtoft village, next forged a course along the valley of the Kilham Road, heading toward Kilham itself, three miles distant.

For the following week the villagers washed and scrubbed their salvaged possessions as best they could in the muddy pools left by the flood. There was no fresh water left in the village as the village well had been filled with mud and the pump washed away. Fresh water in the form of bottled aerated water was ferried from Driffield by Mr F Purdom and a Mr Waind, along with a fleet of requisitioned carriers laden with bread, bacon and tea and other food supplies, emergency clothing, bedding, boots, etc. Eventually the well dried out and was put into use once more. However, initially, until the problem finally solved itself, on operating the pump handle, raw sewage would emerge from the spout, necessitating a voluntary drought throughout the village whenever such unwelcome visitations should occur.

Concerning the subject of the well. Following continued damage to the appliance through flood and seepage, in 1903, it was thought necessary to install a new village pump by the relevant authorities. It was reported at the monthly meeting of the Driffield Rural Council 'that the Parish Council of Langtoft had signified their approval of Mr J Villiers, of Beverley, putting down a new pump at Langtoft, at a cost of £89 10s 6d, and that Mr Villiers had agreed to a recommendation from the Parish Council of Langtoft that he be paid one half of the amount on the completion of the work, and the remainder at the end of twelve months.'[12] Undoubtedly, confidence in the operational capability of any new village pump was uppermost in the minds of the village guardians, hence the delay in final payments to Mr Villier.

In the immediate aftermath of the flood, when the only possible means of conveyance through the flooded areas of the village was by boat, the vicar, the Reverend Thomas Speck, inspected the damage from a small punt. Unfortunately, the reverend gentleman on his tour suffered a blow to the side of the head from one of the oars manipulated by the churchwarden, John Wharram. It is said that the poor oarsman was that day treated to a range of language from the Reverend Speck never to have featured in his services at St Peter's.

On Monday, 4 July, the Reverend Speck made an urgent appeal through the press for contributions in aid of the disaster occasioned by the occurrence of the previous day, and stated that the Driffield banks, along with himself, would receive donations.

A meeting of the parishioners was held on Wednesday of that week to consider the best means of relieving the distress. A general committee was then formed consisting of the following Langtoft persons, George Shipley, John Wilson, William Easby, Mr R Gatenby, S Walker, R Bower, S Featherstone, Joseph Savile and M Slaughter, assisted by H. Holt, CF Sharp, F Purdom and GR Jackson, of Driffield.

Figure 8. Round Hill, showing the effects of the storm damage of 1892.

The Reverend Sharp, Methodist Minister, was appointed treasurer and secretary to the vicar of Langtoft, and a sub-committee was further appointed to carry out the day-to-day business. It was decided to give each of the poorer villagers the sum of ten shillings for their immediate needs, and to issue notices asking those who had suffered from the flood to send in their particulars for adjudication with a view to receiving further payments. Soon after the catastrophe, the vicar distributed two pounds-worth of bread to the needy. The Misses Kingston, of *Kilham West Field Farm*, drove over on the Tuesday with a supply of tea and bread, which was distributed to the people in their homes.

Further assistance was provided by others in various forms, but such was the overwhelming sympathy felt for the people of Langtoft by the countryside as a whole, that the total monetary amount of £1340 18s 5d was collected by subscription.

The following week it is said that thousands of people visited Langtoft and its vicinity in order to witness the destruction, which eye-witnesses recount was far greater than the newspapers actually reported.

It may be noted here that a great body of water from Cottam Hills

Figure 9. A commemorative stone set in the wall of a house in the village that shows the height that the flood waters reached in 1892.

made its way through the intervening sinuous valleys, and at the foot of *Teigho Hill* leading into Langtoft village, had crossed the road, and rushing down the incline had joined the flood-torrent in its exit from Langtoft towards Kilham.

As a consequence of this action, in the deep valley below the steep *Teigho Hill*, was seen for many days, a deep and broad deposit of mud left by the water alluded to, which was of lake-like proportion.

It was written by Mr JD Hood, in his book on the event, *Waterspouts of the Yorkshire Wolds*, 'Few of the thousands of visitors who during the past three months have visited Langtoft could fail to be greatly impressed by what may be termed the key-scene of the disaster.'

Figure 10. Nineteenth century graffiti on the tower of the village church in which many of the residents were attending service on that fateful morning in July 1892.

Toward the end of 1892, the Reverend Jordan Sharp wrote in his Journal:

> *The year has been an eventful one. God in His Mysterious providence visited us with a great flood on Sunday evening, 3 July, but God in His mercy permitted not one life to be lost. Six months have now elapsed but not one, to my knowledge, has taken this visitation of God as a call to prepare to meet their Judge.*

As a postscript, in 1975, whilst work was being carried out at the Chapel, large deposits of solidified flood silt were discovered beneath the Chapel floor.

In the aftermath of the storm, it was seen that two deep channels had appeared on the slopes of *Round Hill* (Figure 8) These extended from near the summit to the bottom of the hill - a distance of about a hundred yards - and were parallel to each other. Each gully then terminated in two holes at the lower end about ten feet in depth and some twelve feet in width. Various theories were propounded to account for these miniature ravines.

Figure 11. The War Memorial, Langtoft village.

Some contended that rents of this description could only be effected by the action of lightning. Others, ignoring altogether the descent of a vertical column of water in the shape of a waterspout, insisted that a chasm of some twelve feet broad at the base and tapering to a point at the apex, could only have been formed by a sheet of water rushing over the summit of the hill, making first a slight aperture which naturally widened and deepened with the force.

It was, however, concluded that the most reasonable conjecture was that a column of water, or 'waterspout' – or possibly two in conjunction – burst on the hillside, forming the large holes and by regurgitation caused a tapering rent, which the surface water then flowing down with some force, would naturally enlarge.

Today, the only evidence of any flooding at Langtoft, is a memorial placed high on a house wall (Figure 9) that records the seventeenth century flood and marks the height that the flood waters reached in 1892.

Notes and References

1. Known hereabouts as High Street and Wold Gate.
2. W Greenwood, *British Barrows*, p.204; Excavation Annual Report, 1966 (HMSO).
3. OS Map 6î (1854).
4. Census, 1951.
5. LANGTOFT is Lang(h)etou 1086 DB, Langetoft 1164-70 Reg Alb et passim to 1386 Test, Lantoft(e) 14th Sawley, 1334 SR et passim to 1521 Test (on the Woold) 1584 Feet of Fines. 'Long piece of ground,' v. land, topt. Lindkvist (219) compares Langetot in Normandy and Dr G. Knudsen calls attention to the Danish place-name Langtoft (DaSN(Sj) iii, 328, etc.).
6. COTTAM Cottun 1086 DB, Cotum 1285 KI, 1295 Ebor, 1306 BevAct, 1316 Nom Vill Cotom 1337, 1376 Feet Of Fines, Cotome 1508 Test, Cottam 1598 FF 'At the cottages,' from Old English cotum, dat. Plur. Of cote. LAMBERT DALE (6î) is Lambcotedayle 12th Malton. V. lamb, bot, deill.
7. EPNS, *Place-Names of ER of Yorkshire & York*, p.96.97.
ibid.
8. Registry of Deeds, 1610/119/100; Local information.
9. Thos Jefferys, *Map of Yorkshire* (1772).
ibid.; C Greenwood, *Map of Yorkshire* (1817).
10. Hull Corporation Records, Bench Book No.5, p495.
11. It was later discovered that two furrows had been gouged out by the waterspout down the flank of the Wold.
12. *Driffield Times*, 1903.

10. Plain Tales from Scalby

by Alan Whitworth

ON 30 NOVEMBER 1979, Miss Florence Mildred Kidd died peacefully in Scarborough hospital. After seventy-eight years of life there was no grieving husband, no children left behind. There was a brother, however, and a nephew and niece, and something else, a small, fat scrapbook, onto whose pages were lovingly written and stuck the history of a lifetime – and more, patiently collected, the history of a village in whose environs Miss Kidd, and her family before then even, had been irrefragably entwined.

Inherited from her mother, the wife of Edwin Kidd, coachman to Mrs J W Rowntree, widow of the Quaker cocoa magnate, who resided in Scalby, and before that, in the employment of Lord Airedale of *Cober Hill*, Cloughton (Figure 1), and later coachman to Mr James A Cooke, proprietor of the Hull News and Hull Daily, the scrapbook was in turn started by her parents in the early- or mid-nineteenth century.

The daughter of Mrs J W Rowntree, Miss Jean Rowntree, corresponded with, and visited 'Milly' Kidd, as she was popularly known to friends in Scalby, up until her end. In turn, and despite their differences in social standing, the spinster visited Miss

Figure 1. Cober Hill, Cloughton, once the home of Sir Frank Lockwood, and later Lord Airedale, and finally now run as an Adult School Guest House by the Society of Friends

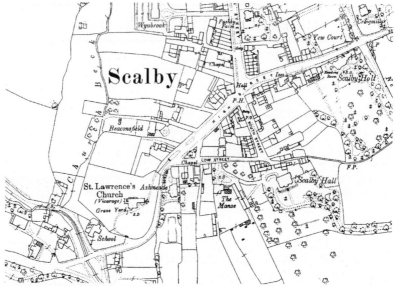

Figure 2. A map of Scalby.

Rowntree at her London home and elsewhere, often holidaying with her and the family too – they were lifetime friends and Miss Rowntree was familiar with the scrapbook, had even borrowed it, writing when she returned it, 'I have enjoyed reading the scrapbook – it is really your family as well as your granny's', adding 'I ought to post it back to you when I get back to the cottage[1] – you won't want to be without it. . .'

How did I come by it, a total stranger?

In truth I rescued it from a York postcard dealer some years back. Possibly on the death of Miss 'Milly' it had passed into the hands of her surviving brother, Henry Francis Kidd, who died in 1986 and lived at Acomb, on the outskirts of York. Perhaps his children overlooked its importance during the sad and tiresome business of sorting his effects, discarding lightly a collection once so proudly cherished through three generations. Whatever the reason, the important fact is that through the Kidd family we are able to put together a picture of Scalby during its most glorious years, when the village flourished as the 'genteel suburb' of Scarborough and attracted a number of eminent men and women of the day (Figure 2). Persons of the calibre of John W Rowntree; Tom Laughton, whose family and later himself, owned a prestigious hotel in Scarborough, and who was brother of the actor Charles Laughton; the Sitwell family; and Will Catlin and his famous 'Pierott' family to name but a few who lived and left their indelible stamp on this oft praised hamlet.

John Cole, the nineteenth century writer, described the village of Scalby as 'seated in a vale, surrounded by ranges of majestic hills, in the wapentake of Pickering-Lythe, in the North Riding of the county of York, distant from Scarborough 3 miles, 40 from York, 18 respectively from Pickering and Whitby, and from London *via* York 237, via Lincoln 211.'[2] He went on to say, 'the situation of Scalby is more pleasant, and its general appearance more inviting, than many other villages of the county; it being agreeably dispersed; not having too much of the straight line, but presenting many rural deviations, both as regards the buildings themselves and their situation (Figure 3)'.[3]

The *Victoria County History* records that Scalby parish was composed in 1831 of the townships of Burniston, Cloughton, Newby, Scalby, Staintondale and Throxenby. The area of this parish was given as 11,759 acres of land, 380 acres of foreshore and 18 acres of inland water.[4] By 1890 the parish had been reduced to the townships of Scalby and Throxenby, the new area of the whole being 3,992 acres and the population numbering 802; of this, the township of Scalby itself contained 2,730 acres (including 126 acres of sea coast) and held 600 inhabitants,[5] a figure unchanged from 1857[6] and 1859[7] but which had risen steadily from 446 in 1823,8 to 583 in the year 1840.[9] Today I doubt if the figure is much altered.

The Kidd family came to Scalby in 1883. They came, Henry and Hannah, with three children, to their employer's newly built house, *The Holt*. Henry Kidd had been coachman with Mr A J Cooke for over fifteen years by then. They had come from Hull, at least that is where their youngest child, Edwin had been born about the time

Figure 3. Looking along North Street into South Street. The former Temperance Hall stands on the corner (left) with Sedman's Butchers in the foreground (left). Opposite on the right is the Nags Head public house, then under the ownership of Laughton, who once lived in Scalby. In the far centre background is the village shop, run by Rowntree's.

Henry had come into service with Mr Cooke. Indeed, at the date Edwin came to Scalby, he was old enough to take a position himself as coachman with Mr Cooke, working alongside his father (Figure 4), a satisfactory arrangement all round, and one which undoubtedly showd the regard with which Mr Cooke held Henry Kidd, for Edwin's elder brother, Charles Thomas, was also recently in the employ of Mr Cooke, on the staff of his newspaper, The *Hull Daily News.* Their middle child and only daughter, Frances Hannah, it appears, stayed at home and helped mother run the house, which at that time, was *Holt Cottage,* set aside by Mr Cooke for the use of the coachman and his family.

Their mother Hannah, was a native of Bridlington, the youngest of twelve children. She was born in 1837, the year Queen Victoria came to the throne. Her father, John Warley, was a brewer in the town (Figure 5). Little is known of him except that a short

Figure 4. Edwin Kidd in 1926, possibly seated in his own front room at 4 Jubilee Terrace.

handwritten note penned after his death stated how:

A Queen Elizabeth shilling was dug up in a garden at Bridlington

Figure 5. A typical brewery yard in the nineteenth century as might be known to Hannah Kidd, whose father John Warley, was a brewer in Bridlington.

dated 1566 in the year 1866 by John Warley, brewer, of Bridlington, just 300 hundred years old, and [is] now in the possession of his daughter Hannah Kidd in Scalby, 1921. The Queen's effigy was very clear.

A number of years later in February 1937, this was reprinted with additions in the local newspaper:

A discussion on old coins has been taking place in our columns recently, and Mr Edwin Kidd, of 2 Curraghmore Terrace, Scalby, informs us that he has in his possession a shilling of the reign of Queen Elizabeth I, dated 1566. This was dug up by his grandfather while working in his garden at the back of the old Priory Church, Bridlington, over 100 years ago. It is in a good state of preservation.

John Warley had at least one brother, Henry, and one sister. She married Captain William Scott, of Hull, and an offspring of their union, the eldest, William Henry, cousin to Hannah, was drowned on 16 February 1879, when the *SS Jura*, of Glasgow, sank on the Yarmouth Cross Sands. At the time the steamship met its untimely end on a regular voyage between Hull, Cyprus and Smyrna, William Henry was first mate, aged thirty-five, of Russell Street, Hull.

A newspaper cutting, one of three accounts pasted in the family album recalls in detail the supposed fate of the *SS Jura* and its crew of eighteen mainly crew sailors.

The following is the report of William Snook, water-clerk of Messrs Turrill and Torkildsen, of Great Yarmouth:- Deponent was called up at 4am on February 17, in consequence of signals having been seen on the Cross Sand, and finding the steamtug Pilot going out, went on board and proceeded from Yarmouth at 5am. At 6.30am, tide being half flood, weather hazy, wind NE, blowing light with a heavy swell of sea from the NE, the steamtug having previously spoken to the St Nicholas Lightship, the master of which stated that he seen no signal of distress, proceeded to the eastward of Cross Sand, and cruised about till daylight, when at 7.30am they fell in with a quantity of wreckage, apparently of a steamer, there being the greater part of the poop (half round), hatches, and other portions of the deck of a steamer. The tug steamed amongst the wreckage, and they saw two boats, and took one in tow which was full of water, and left the other, which was too much damaged. The boat was marked, 'SS Jura, Glasgow'. They also picked up a medicine chest marked the same.

Henry Warley, John's only brother we know about, lived at *Pasture*

House, in Beeford, in the East Riding. He had a number of children, and two daughters it is recorded, married: Sarah Ann, second daughter, on 5 February 1891, at the Priory Church, Bridlington, by the Reverend Dr Given, to Joseph Sugden, of Huddersfield; and Mary, third daughter, on 23 September the year previous, at the village church of St Paul, Beeford, by the Reverend L W Higgins, vicar of Foston, to John Alfred Wilcox, of Scarborough.

Henry Kidd was born at Ellerker, a small village in the East Riding. From what size family he came we are not told, but it would appear that he had at least a sister, as a nephew of the same name as his father, was somewhat of a poet, and on the death of his father's employer, he had published a eulogy entitled 'Lines Composed by Isaac Swinton, Jun, *addressed to his Father, Gardener at Manby Hall,* on the Death of his late Master, W T Welfit, Esq. who Died on the 25 of January, 1864.' The copy which was lovingly preserved in the family album had a handwritten note that read, *nephew of Henry Kidd, Scalby.*

It would appear that Henry's own early employment was at *Ellerker Hall* as coachman, as there survives an altered and dated steel engraving taken from a magazine of the time of a coach and horses shown on its journey from the Hall (Figure 6). On leaving there the

Figure 6. A steel engraving showing a picture of a coach and horses and that has been altered by Henry Kidd who was a coachman at Ellerker Hall.

family still took an interest in the property and an advertisement published on the sale of *Ellerker Hall*, describes the extent and nature of the estate as they knew it:

Ellerker Hall Estate, East Yorkshire
TO BE SOLD BY AUCTION
By Mr W N Lewendon

At the Royal Station Hotel, Hull, on TUESDAY, August 30th, at Half-Past Two for Three o'clock in the afternoon, subject to such conditions as shall be then read, and which may be seen on application to the auctioneer, or to the undermentioned solicitors, three days prior to the sale.

ALL that capital Freehold country RESIDENCE, known by the name of 'Ellerker Hall' situated at Ellerker in the East Riding of the County of York, containing Entrance-Hall, three Reception-rooms, four principal and other Bed-rooms, newly fitted Bath and Lavatory with hot and cold water, good Kitchens, Butler's Pantry and other conveniences, together with Stabling for six horses, good Harness-rooms, newly erected Coach-house which will hold four carriages, Wash-house, Cow-house, Piggery, Hen-house, excellent Kitchen Garden well stocked with fruit trees, tastefully laid out Ornamental Pleasure Garden with Croquet Lawn, two Green-houses and Vinery, and the newly-erected Gothic Lodge.

ALSO all those four grass PADDOCKS, two of which are situate in front of the Hall (enclosed with iron fence), and two at the back, having extensive frontages to the highroads.

ALSO all that COTTAGE and plot of Freehold LAND, containing 23 perches or thereabouts, situated in the village of Ellerker aforesaid, now in the occupation of Mr Thomas Sparks, which cottage is now used as a post-office, and also those Two COTTAGES or TENEMENTS and Garden, situate in the village of Ellerker, now in the occupations of Messrs Tidbrook and Rogers. These last-mentioned premises are copyhold of the Manor of Howden.

The whole of the above Estate is now held by Henry Smith, Esquire, and his under-tenants, at the very low rental of £110 per annum, and comprises and area of 11 acres or thereabouts. The Residence is approached by a half-circle carriage drive with double entrance gates. There is an excellent supply of pure water. It is thickly and very ornamentally timbered and surrounded by a beautiful and well-wooded country, not far distant from the River Humber, and is worthy the attention of anyone seeking a desirable country residence.

Any purchaser not requiring the whole of the land and cottages might let part off for about £40 per annum, without detriment to the residence and pleasure grounds.

Ellerker Hall is within 15 minutes drive of the Brough Station, on the North-Eastern Railway, and is about 11/2 miles from Cave and the new station of the Hull and Barnsley Railway.

(a)

Later, Henry held a position at *Burton Constable Hall,* seat of the Chichester-Constable family. Indeed, it is very probable that it was here Henry met Hannah his wife-to-be, who was possibly in service too, coming from nearby Bridlington.

There is no record of when they married, but it would be around this time, and a number of items dated in the late 1850s confirm their employment at *Burton Constable Hall,* and include an extensive account of the twenty-first birthday celebrations of Mr (Lieutenant) Raleigh Chichester-Constable which records that apart from the main celebrations for three hundred invited distinguished guests from 'all parts of the County. . . The tenants on the East Riding estate and tradesmen were similarly entertained last evening, and for Boxing Day the servants and staff have been invited to a ball.' There is an embossed invitation card bearing the family arms and the title 'Burton Constable', dated 23 February 1857, which gives a list of dances to another festive occasion (Figure 7). Elsewhere, other celebratory events are recorded in the form of two printed handbills displaying separate theatrical productions at

(b)

Figure 7(a) & (b). An embossed invitation card for a dance held at Burton Constable Hall, showing on the reverse a list of dances performed.

the 'Theatre Royal, Burton Constable' on the evenings of 27 and 28 March 1856, when servants and staff were entertained by the family and friends playing the roles of 'servants' in two farces – *Unfinished Gentleman* and *High Life below Stairs*. Indeed, it would seem that despite the hard work expected, for those in service there was never a dull moment and much 'high life below stairs'.

The eldest son of Henry and Hannah, Charles Thomas Kidd, married, and the couple first lived in Scalby. In 1902, however, they left the village for Hull. Friends and colleagues of Mrs Kidd held her in high esteem and a presentation was arranged prior to her departure that was recorded in the local newspaper:

An interesting gathering of the Scalby branch of the Mothers' Union was held in the Temperance hall, Scalby on Thursday evening. This branch of the society, under the able management of Miss Barker, the Hon Secretary, has for some years past done excellent work in providing and making garments for Dr Barnado's Home, and one of its most energetic members is Mrs Kidd, who has been a well-known and much-respected resident of the village for nearly twenty years. Mrs Kidd is now leaving Scalby to take up her residence in Hull, and members and associates of the Mothers' Union testified the esteem and regard in which she has been so deservedly held by them by presenting her with a very handsome solid silver sugar basin, of Queen Anne pattern, bearing the inscription, 'Presented to Mrs Kidd by members of the Scalby branch of the Mothers' Union, 1902'. The presentation was made on behalf of the subscribers by the vicar of Scalby (the Rev W Cautley Robinson), who in a few well-chosen words expressed the general regret which is felt at the departure from Scalby of Mrs Kidd, who has always been an active worker in every parochial movement. Mrs Kidd having responded, the meeting terminated.

Sadly, their move to Hull was short-lived. On 26 June the following year Charles Thomas died, and from the printed obituary it appears his wife by this date, had also passed away as no account mentions a bereaved widow left to grieve, nor, does it seem was there any issue of their union.

Aged forty-two years he '... died very suddenly... Mr Kidd was on holiday at Cloughton where his brother resides, and up to within an hour of his death, which was due to sudden heart failure, he was in his usual and cheerful spirits... [He] was for many years associated with the staff of the *Hull News*, havng entered the office as a lad. He was the son of the late Mr Henry Kidd, of Scalby, formerly of

Figure 8. St Laurences church, Scalby

Ellerker, and for many years in the employ of Mr J A Cooke, the proprietor of the *Hull News*. Mr Kidd the younger, continued with the latter as clerk and bookkeeper up to the time of the amalgamation in 1898 of the *Hull News* with the present company, to whom his services were transferred, and with whom he remained up to the time of his death.

Some time ago he was laid aside for several months with a severe illness, and returned to business about eighteen months ago. He was last week away on holiday with his brother, who resides at Cloughton [*Cober Hill*], when on Friday night he was taken ill and passed away within the hour.

Mr Kidd was of a quiet unobtrusive nature and kindly disposition. He was most trustworthy, and possessed the confidence and esteem of his employers, by whom as well as by all his colleagues, he was highly respected. His sudden and unexpected death is greatly deplored.

The funeral took place on Monday in the picturesque churchyard of Scalby, near Scarborough (Figure 8). The chief mourners were the deceased's mother, brother, and sister, and there were also present Mr A Tidman (representing Mr J O'Hara the editor-manager of the *Eastern Morning* and *Hull News* company) and MR W Stalker (cashier) who placed on the coffin a wreath sent by the deceased's fellow-employees. There were several other floral devices, including one from Mrs J A Cooke.

The service was impressively conducted by the Rev W C Robinson (vicar of Scalby), assisted by the Rev J T Tause (vicar of Cloughton),

Figure 9. Jubilee Terrace, as it appears today, still very much an untouched Victorian terrace.

the former in the church paying a high tribute to the personal qualities of Mr Kidd.'

Frances Hannah, the beloved and only daughter of the late Henry Kidd and Mrs Kidd, of *4 Jubilee Terrace,* Scalby, passed away 27 January 1915 (Figure 9). She remained unmarried and died aged forty-nine years.

Their youngest son, Edwin Warley Kidd, was the only one to survive, marry and produce children, and live to see grandchildren. Born in 1867, he died after a short illness in 1941 aged seventy-four. Edwin's address at his date of death was given as 2 Curraghmore Terrace, Scalby which he possibly took at the time of his retirement in 1925 when leaving his employment at *Low Hall.* His first period of work was in the service of Mr J A Cooke, of *Scalby Halt,* as coachman, working first alongside his father Henry. It was during this time, that Edwin and Lousia Kidd's first child, Henry Francis was born on 13 March 1898 (Figure 10). It is not known, however, when Edwin married his wife, nor the circumstance of their meeting. Not long afterwards, Edwin moved his employment and family to Lord Airedale, at *Cober Hill,* Cloughton, businessman and newspaper magnate. It was while working

Figure 10. Henry Francis Kidd.

Figure 11. Lousia Ellen Kidd, mother of Henry Frances and 'Milly' Kidd. It was her mother Hannah, who began the family album.

here that his brother Charles died on a visit in 1903 – two years after the birth of Edwin's second child, a daughter, baptised Florence Mildred 'Milly' in the church of St Laurence, Scalby, in November 1901, wherein Edwin Kidd was sidesman for many years.

Nine years later, Edwin returned to Scalby, and took up his final employment in the service of the widow of Mr John W Rowntree, the cocoa and chocolate manufacturer of York and social reformer. Mrs J W Rowntree lived at *Low Hall,* built by them and later taken over by the Miner's Welfare Fund as a convalescent home (Figure 12).

Edwin Kidd's father, Henry Kidd died in 1896, never seeing his grandchildren. His short obituary reveals little of the man who died while still in service with Mr J A Cooke:

It is not often that a village funeral attracts so large an attendance of sympathetic friends, and spectators as was witnessed on Tuesday at the internment of Henry Kidd, for twenty-four years the valued servant and valued coachman of Mr J A Cooke. The service was conducted, in the absence of the Vicar, by the Rev T W T Hart, MA, Rector of St Cuthbert's, Hawick, Scotland. At the conclusion of the portion of the service read in church, Mr hart gave a brief address, in which he said that the chief object in life was to discover and lead the true religious life, the Christianity which Christ taught. What was that life? It consisted of two things, and neither was complete without the other: Devotion to God; duty towards man. That, and that alone, comprehended the entirety of religion. This great object of life their

Figure 12. Low Hall, Scalby built by John Rowntree. It was here that Milly grew up and became friends with Jean, the daughter of Mr and Mrs J W Rowntree.

brother whose remains they were now committing to peaceful rest had sought for, and attained in large measure. For nearly a quarter of a century, respected and esteemed by all who knew him, Henry Kidd had been a valued servant to his employer. In these days of constant, restless, ever changing service that was a noteworthy fact. Such a period tended inevitably to gradually efface the ordinary distinction of master and servant, to raise the latter into the position of a valued and trustworthy friend, whose advice on matters within his own special experience was esteemed. Their departed brother was a man whose religion was as earnest as it was retiring. He loved his Church, and, when ill-health forbade his attendance there, always followed the appointed service for the day in his Prayer Book. It was surely with something more than hope that they would now lay him in the quiet precincts of that hallowed ground.

Henry's widow, Hannah Kidd, went on to outlive her husband by thirty years. On his death, she took up residence at *4 Jubilee Terrace*, living with her daughter, Frances, until the latter's death in 1915, then alone until 1926 when Hannah herself died, aged eighty-nine, well remembered and well respected in the village and 'one of Scalby's oldest residents'. On her death it was recorded that 'since just before Christmas Mrs H Kidd. . . had been in ill-health, and on the Monday afternoon she passed away at the above address'. At the time of her passing, Hannah still had a sister (one of twelve) residing at Bridlington, aged ninety-four. 'Mrs Kidd took a great deal of interest in the village Church life, and in earlier years was a regular attender at the services.'

A year later, an issue of the parish magazine contained the following tribute to the above:

'Life's race well run' may be truly said at the passing of Hannah Kidd. Full of years – she would have been ninety on 6 February – held in high esteem by friends and acquaintances, a good and zealous churchwoman, with unflagging zeal in good works, she has entered into the rest of Paradise, where her works have followed her. It is given to few in her station of life to enjoy and employ so fully the faculties of mind and body. A real 'Mother in Israel'. A pattern indeed for latter-day mothers to emulate, if they would command the love and duty of their children.'

Never remarrying, Hannah Kidd herself coming from a large family, was related through marriage into an even larger one – the Abram family. This family was one of distinction in the neighbourhood, and through this connection, was a member of an enormous 'extended' family that reached all parts of Yorkshire and beyond as can be seen in this obituary:

> *The funeral of the late Mrs Abram took place on Saturday* [29 December 1923: died 26 December]. *A service was held in the Wesleyan Chapel at 2.30pm, conducted by Mr T Barrett and Rev W Hesmondhalgh, Vicar of Scalby. There was a large gathering of relatives and friends an evidence of the love and respect for Mrs Abram by all who knew her. Out of her fifteen sons and daughters, it is believed that thirteen were present at the funeral. The hymn, 'Jesu, Lover of my Soul' and 'Rock of Ages' were sung during the service. There were many beautiful floral tributes of love. On Sunday evening a special memorial service was held in the Wesleyan Chapel in memory of the late Mrs Abram, conducted by Mr R Frankish. Mrs Abram was the oldest member of the church, having reached the age of eighty-three. She became a member of Mr Severs' class when she first came to live at Scalby and has taken a delight in attending the services when she was able. There was a good attendance of friends and relatives at the service. . .*

She and her husband, Francis Abram (b.1823), son of a well-established family in Burniston, formerly carried on a dairy business at *Cockrah Farm*, and afterwards removed to *Clarence House*, Burniston. Mr Abram's father, John Abram and his wife, lived at one time in the house once occupied by Mr W Lee, and in a full and rewarding life, were witnesses at the trial that followed the dramatic shooting tragedy at Burniston in February 1823 (see 'The Smugglers Revenge'). Before moving into Burniston, they lived for a period at *Yew Court*, Scalby, before financial constraints forced them to move (Figure 13).

At the time of Mr and Mrs Francis Abram's golden wedding anniversary in 1908, they had fifteen children – twelve daughters and three sons – all of whom survive and married, except two, and there was a total of forty grandchildren! Three of the daughters resided at Scarborough, one being Mrs Crawford, wife of the caretaker of Gladstone Road Schools, and another the wife of the coachman

Figure 13. Yew Court, Scalby, once the home of Mr & Mrs Abram, and later the home of Will Catlin the Scarborough Pierott.

of Mr Kirk, brewer. One daughter, the wife of Mr Tindall, blacksmith, lived at Harwood Dale, two resided at Burniston, one at Bishop Auckland, one at Harrogate, one at Sutton, and another lived at Terrington. Two further sons and a daughter resided near Leeds.

Francis Abram married his bride Ann at Scalby parish church on 18 December 1858, even though it was said that he was born and lived his whole life in Burniston. The ceremony was conducted by the Reverend Sedgwick. At the time of their golden wedding fifty years on, when Mrs Abram was sixty-eight and her husband seventy-five, it was reported that Mrs Abram regularly walked into Scarborough each market day. The occasion of their anniversary was honoured by the presentation of a purse of gold by their children.

Meanwhile, Henry Francis (Figure 14) and Florence Mildred (Figure 15), the children of Edwin and Louisa Kidd, were growing up in Scalby. Henry was born at *Holt Cottage* while his father worked for Mr James A Cooke. At the outbreak of the 1914-18 hostilities, he was of an age to be 'called up' and served in France.

It is not known what became of Henry on his return from the war, the only newspaper cutting is an account of his wedding at St Mary's parish church, Scarborough, undated, which recalls his marriage to Marguerite (Madge) daughter of Mr and Mrs A Thornton, of 45 Newborough, Scarborough.

The Rev Watts officiated at the ceremony. The bride, who was given away by her father, was attired in a dress of mauve crepe-de-chine and grey shoes, with hat to match. She carried a bouquet of lilies and roses and was attended by two bridesmaids, Miss Freda Thornton (sister of the bride) and Miss Mildred Kidd (sister of the bridegroom) who wore dresses of camelia taffeta silk, with black hats. Their bouquets consisted of gladiolas and irises. The best man was Mr E Good, of Scarborough. They were the recipients of many presents, amongst which was a very pretty clock, presented by the Scalby Church Choir, of which the bridegroom has been a member for thirteen years. The happy pair left for Llandudno, where the honeymoon is being spent.

Later the couple moved to York, undoubtedly for Henry's employment, possibly with Messrs Leake and Thorpe, of Coney Street, whose original premises dramatically burnt down in January 1933, and were rebuilt on the site over some nine months following the demolition of

Figure 14. Henry Francis Kidd (1898-1986) grandson of Henry Kidd of Scalby and formerly of Ellerker. His father was Edwin W Kidd.

Figure 15. Florence 'Milly' Kidd (1901-79)

the remains in June of the same year.

Henry, four years older than his sister, outlived Florence, and died suddenly at Scarborough while on a visit from his home at Acomb, near York. His wife it appears died before him (Figure 16). He left two children, Margaret (born at a York Nursing Home) and David, both of whom married and produced grandchildren – Sally, Alison, Joanna and Philippa.

Florence Mildred Kidd remained at Scalby, living with her mother at *33 North Street*, unmarried. As a child 'Milly' first attended the local village school before later entering the roll of Gladstone Road school, Scarborough, 'cycling in each day' recalled Jean Rowntree, daughter of Mrs J W Rowntree, and a lifelong friend.

In later years they corresponded frequently and regularly, particularly when Miss Rowntree moved away from Scalby to Kent, while retaining a cottage at Brandsby, and many postcards survive giving a picture of Milly's 'daily round' in old age. Much later still, Jean Rowntree was instrumental in assisting Milly gain a place at Ravensworth Lodge, Belgrave Crescent, Scarborough, a residential nursing home owned by the York Friend's Housing Society, a Quaker organisation, and given to them by Joseph Rowntree, brother of John W Rowntree, both of whom were staunch Quakers, as was their father and the Rowntree family for centuries. Before that time, however, Milly was most active, even travelling to Switzerland with friends in 1972, while in her seventy-first year of age.

From: Home Farm Cottage, Brandsby, Yorkshire. 2 August 1972.
This is a quick one to say that it looks as if we could come over to Scalby on Tuesday 8th. We have been a bit held up because of Anthea, who hasn't long left before she goes back to Australia but keeps changing her plans. We would look in at the end of the morning. NOT for a meal! But if Tuesday is not convenient, Ben & I could come later, after Mammie [Poore] goes home – we shall be here 2 more weeks. I hope this allows you long enough to let us know. We are in most evenings after 7 (except Monday) if you would rather telephone. Let's hope for better weather.

Best wishes, Jean R.

From: Home Farm Cottage, Brandsby, Yorkshire. 10 August 1972.
This is just to thank you for your hospitality on Tuesday. I do hope you got your own lunch SOMETIME! Also to say how much we enjoyed your Marmalade Ginger Bread – I do think it was kind of you to make it – and looking at your cards. Annie asked to be remembered to you & she has a lovely little jersey cow called Rosie which is quite spoilt & wants to be the centre of attention. Its butter, which we had on our bread for tea, was like what we used to have at Low Hall. Next year you must come to Whole Farm in spring. PS I thought this card might interest you.

Best wishes from us all, Jean R.

Figure 16. A family group at the silver wedding (29 September 1954) of Henry F Kidd and his wife Madge (nee Marguerite Thornton) with Milly (left).

The postcard in question was a sepia reproduction of a Frank Meadow Sutcliffe photograph showing corn-ricks being built, entitled, 'The Ingathering'; with a caption stating, 'Taken around 1895 at *Four Lane Ends Farm*, Whitby. At one time a tollgate was part of the farm through which Bonnie Prince Charlie is reputed to have passed one stormy night.'

From: Ponteland, Northumberland. 24 September 1972. Thank you for your postcard & message. Hope you have enjoyed your visit to Redcar, & all your other visits too. Haven't seen you since Cup Final day with me – Oh! I remember, on a seat opposite the library that day. I've had rather a queer summer. Cousins with me, then back for a week at Mellor Brook as they had an empty back seat. Betty suggested my going & George brought me back. But I picked up a virus in B'burn [Blackburn?] & became ill after I got home! Better now & staying up here for a welcome change & good company. I think you will like this sunset view of the Northumberland coast [Beaddnell Bay]. It's a lovely country. Hope you are well.

Love from Doris.

Figure 17. Milly Kidd (centre back) and friends at Harewood House, near Leeds, 24 May 1950

From: Sheffield, South Yorkshire. 25 October 1972.
Dear Aunty Millie, Thank you for your letter this week. We shall be coming to Scarborough on Monday 30 October & would like to come & see you. We'll come in the morning probably about 11. If you will be away or it's not convenient let me know. We shall be having lunch in Scarborough.

Love Judy & David, J[oanna] & P[hilippa]'

These are brother Henry Kidd's daughter and son-in-law, and their children.

From: Whole Farm, Stone-in-Oxney, Kent. 13 November 1973.
Many thanks for your card – I had a lovely birthday (mostly spent gardening). This is to say that we should like to get you an electric iron for Christmas, but I thought I had better write first to ask if you had one already, & also if you really prefer not to be bothered with it! I think you CAN get the kind where the ironing board plugs in, & you don't have to have a dangling flex on the iron – but I am not sure. Do you remember being hemmed in parking at the place on this card [High Street, Tenterden, Kent] & nearly missing the train?

Best wishes, Jean R.

From: York. 23 March 1975. I bought this card at London Zoo. We had a super day and arrived home at 11pm very tired. The football match was great, England won 4-0. It was a long day, we left York at 6.20am but it was worth it. Thank you for the postcard.

Love from Alison [Henry Kidd's granddaughter]

From: Home Farm Cottage, Brandsby, Yorkshire. 14 April 1975[?].
Thank you so much for your letter & the interesting enclosures: I especially like the one about holidays in Scarborough. We were rather late arriving here as I stayed on an extra day in London hoping to see Tony, but there were no trains running & no one could say when there would be, so we had to come up without managing it. This is just to say that we hope to come to Scalby sometime between 22nd & 26th April – AFTER your weekend at David's – I will have to let you know which day later on (it depends on Sarah's plans) but I thought I had better tell you that it won't be this week. I should be very grateful if you could tell me, when we come, if anyone will be taking on Mr Addison's work on the graves, I have a idea that I owe him for last year, & don't know what to do about it? The weather is still pretty miserable but we manage to get out. All news later.

Best wishes, Jean R.

From: Home Farm Cottage, Brandsby, Yorkshire. 19 April 1975[?].
This is just to ask if Friday (April 25th) would be a possible day for
us to look in on you? I have been waiting to hear from Annie Foster,
but Norah has shingles very badly & I don't think we ought to go
there at all. Not because it is catching – it isn't – but because I know
from experience how any little exertion or even talking to people can
make it worse. However, I do want to see you & talk about plans, &
also see the graves. If it is a fine day we should LIKE to go back via
Langdale End & get in a walk, so we could look in for a REALLY
LIGHT PICNIC LUNCH ABOUT 12.30? NO SPECIAL
PREPARATIONS, just an egg and a cup of tea! If you would rather
telephone than write, we are always here up to 10am or after 7pm
(except on Thursday).

Best wishes, Jean R.

From: Home Farm Cottage, Brandsby, Yorkshire. 26 April
1975[?]. We went here yesterday [Postcard of Fountains Abbey]. I had
forgotten what a lovely place it is. I expect you know it, but we thought
we might take you there in August or September for a picnic if you
can't come to us in Kent.

It was lovely to see you last week. I thought you looked a bit washed
out, and hope your iron tablets will really do you good, & that you
won't hesitate to ask your doctor for something stronger (such as iron
injections) if you don't feel better quite soon. Meanwhile I am
enclosing something to help with the home help. I am sure you won't
want to have one permanently. But I think you might find it worth
trying for the next few weeks while you are having treatment, & I
expect Mrs Lee knows better than I could, how to set about getting
someone.

All good wishes, Jean R.

From: Home Farm Cottage, Brandsby, Yorkshire. 28 April 1975.
Before we leave here (first thing tomorrow) I just wanted to thank you
for a lovely lunch on Friday. I hope it wasn't too awkward having us
the same day as Henry – I wonder how he got on in London? I didn't
even see who won the match.

We also wanted to say that if you don't mind the journey (& the price
of travelling) & don't mind not knowing which of the July dates it
would be, for a little longer of course we should really RATHER you
got to Whole Farm. It would be more of a change for you. But we

should quite understand if you thought it was too much effort & too expensive.

All good wishes from us both. Looking forward to seeing you SOMEWHERE this summer. Jean R.

Undoubtedly this postcard reads in connection with one previous dated 23 March 1975, from Alison, brother Henry Kidd's granddaughter, who gives the result of the England football match, seen while on a visit to London (Wembley?) obviously with granddad Henry.

From: Whole Farm, Stone-in-Oxney, Kent. 2 May 1975.
We got back yesterday – cuckoos singing, and pansies out, but the garden very DRY! We shall have to hoe & water. We found a message, giving us the July dates, waiting & we now see that we shall have no visitors between July 6th & 11th or 12th. The only trouble is that this would mean you travelling on Saturday – (15th). If you can get a reserved seat it would be alright, & Miss Poore will meet you & put you on the train to Ashford on Sunday (6th). This would mean 5 nights here & you could either go straight through on Friday 11th or spend a night in London & leave on Saturday. I am so sorry we can" fit our visitors so that you could travel midweek. Let me know sometime what you think.

Best wishes, Jean R.

From: Whole Farm, Stone-in-Oxney, Kent. 13 May 1975.
Thank you so much for your letter. WE should have thanked YOU for a splendid lunch. I have written direct to Mr Addison & hope that is satisfactory. I have also written to Jessie about holiday plans & will let you know when I hear. I have been rather slow about letters as I have had flu & can't seem to shake it off – it has been hanging on for 10 days now & as soon as I feel better & go out it comes back on my chest again. OLD NAMES OF SCALBY ROADS. The only one I can think of is FOULSYKE (over what used to be the Ford going towards Wrea Head). We have some splendid asparagus & gooseberries & the first roses are out – lovely weather, but we need rain badly. PS I have never seen this bay so empty [Postcard of The Bay, Rye].

Best wishes, Jean R.

From:Whole Farm, Stone-in-Oxney, Kent. 21 June 1975.
I have been meaning to write to you ever since I got your letter about the earthquake – however you will realise by now we weren't in it! Though we did in fact feel the tremour when we were going through the Alps in the train that night. We got quite a shaking, & wondered what on earth was happening.

This is one of the places we must take you to see [Chilham Castle] – you can't go round the house, but there is a beautiful garden. It is a very pretty village. We are very much looking forward to seeing you, & I have first had an answer from Jessie, saying that she hopes to be able to get away for a night or two to join us – she is going to try and arrange it & will let me know for certain later. Miss Poore is looking forward to having you on the 20th July – She may not be able to drive you down next day. But she will put you on the train if not. I will write about train times etc early in July.

Best wishes, Jean R.

From:Whole Farm, Stone-in-Oxney, Kent. 4 July 1975.
Thank you so much for your letter. It is good of Henry [Kidd] to say he would travel with you to Kings Cross. I have heard from Jessie that she thinks she can manage July 24th-26th, & I expect she would travel back with you on the Monday. The only thing is that unless it gets cooler by then - & surely it must do so soon! – I feel it would be a terribly tiring journey for you, & not even a very good time for a visit. We have Miss Schilling here now – she [was] meant to be here with Mrs Stanley – but Mrs Stanley has a bad heart and isn't allowed to travel in the heat (London is like an oven). She is waiting in the hopes of a break in the weather & is really only able to lie about in the shade & occasionally go to the sea. It is really too hot for picnics. Also we have to spend 2 hours every day, while we are still allowed to, trying to keep our vegetables watered. We have had NO rain since February & the garden is like a desert. Let us hope for a change soon – if not I feel perhaps we ought to postpone your visit for a bit? What do you think?

Best wishes, Jean R.

From: Home Farm Cottage, Brandsby,Yorkshire. 2 August 1975.
I wonder how you are feeling now that the weather has got cooler? We got here this weekend – it has got cooler in the south too, but never a drop of rain yet, & no sign of it – everything spoilt & dried up and no hoses allowed for watering.

What we wondered was if you feel like joining us for a picnic – we could come over with a packed lunch, have a drive somewhere, & tea out, & take you back. We could EITHER do a runner up the coast & back by Harwood Dale OR go to Flamborough for our picnic & on to look at Burton Constable (I am not sure which days it is open to the public) & then put you on a train or bus, say at Seamer or Ayon if you were able to change at Scarorough. I thought I would let you think it over in good time to write. If you would rather write than telephone, our best days would be 9th,10th or 11th August (Mon, Tues or Wed) but we could probably do Friday 6th if it suited you better. We would come over about 12 or soon after (I want to see Mrs James first) & bring you, or even get you back after tea. I hope we can manage something; but not if it would hurt your leg.

Best wishes, Jean R.

From: Home Farm Cottage, Brandsby, Yorkshire. 10 August 1975.
I think we would have looked down on [Lake] Gormire last September, on our way back from Scawton?
This is really to say, though I am up here for a time, I have to go back to London because of an abscess in a tooth, which means leaving earlier than we had meant. However we are coming back in September (when we should have been abroad) & I know Mary Jones will want to go over to Scalby & Langdale one day, so I thought I should find out if you are likely to be away between September 10th & 20th? I know you were thinking of going to Margaret's sometime. I wonder how your expedition to the Dales went, OK? & how are you standing this weather – it is a lot hotter here than in Kent – I think the sea cools us down there. It is all right if you can get on top of the moors or into the sea! We had all the Balmes to their evening meal here on Sarah's birthday – enjoyed it very much until we found we had laid the table (in the garden) at the entrance to a wasp's nest. I have Con coming to dinner tonight – she is staying in Haxby.

Best wishes, Jean R.

From: Home Farm Cottage, Brandsby, Yorkshire. 12 August 1975.
Thank you so much for your letter & sending the recipe – I must try it when I bake next. I thought you would like this old view of Rievaulx; also wanted to tell you a coincidence. We were talking to Ashley yesterday (he comes in for a can of beer & a gossip, & does very little gardening while he is about it) and we told him where we had been & he said he had been a garden boy (6/- a week) at Burton

Constable Hall for years – it was his first job! So he was really interested to hear about your grandparents. Though of course that would be before his time – I think he was there just before the 1914 war. I would love to see your scrapbook sometimes – perhaps when we come in September. We will let you know in good time. I am sorry you had trouble with the bus. I am afraid you must have got rather tired. We got our meal at 8.45pm which was quite good going. We did enjoy the day. Looking forward to another one soon.

Jean R.

From: Cockpit Hall, Gillamoor, Yorkshire. 18 August 1976.
Thank you for the money you sent me and Jo. Today we are going to the cinema to see 'It Shouldn't Happen to a Vet'. We have been to Knaresborough and Flamingo Park [Zoo]. On Friday we are going for a picnic in the country. Hope you are well.

Love from Pip & Joanna [Jean Rowntree's niece, Sarah's children].

During late August, it appears Milly took ill, possibly the result of an accident, probably a fire brought on by carelessness in old age which partially destroyed her home and she spent some time in hospital. From the tone of subsequent letters below, it was from this period that Milly's decline became permanent to the extent that later, it was necessary for her to leave Scalby for a place at Ravensworth Lodge, in Belgrave Crescent, Scarborough.

From: Home Farm Cottage, Brandsby, Yorkshire. 4 September 1976.
We are just packing up for an early start tomorrow, but I thought I would send you a line before we go to say how pleased I was to hear from both Henry & Mrs Lee that they had found you better this week. I think you were ready for a good long rest. If you eat well and get out a bit and don't worry, I am quite sure you will soon be home again, perhaps not at 33 North Street, but at some little place in Scalby where there is almost no work. And don't worry about the clean-up either – there are plenty of people to help – if necessary I would come up for 2 or 3 days myself as I am used to cleaning up, & you would be surprised what things auctioneers will take – your old 'blackout' curtains you were telling me about are just the sort of thing. But do get your name down SOON for a bungalow. I asked our friend Kate Mahoney to let us know how you are & if there is anything you want. All good wishes for your complete recovery.

Jean R.

From: Whole Farm, Stone-in-Oxney, Kent. 5 September 1976.
I have just heard from Jessie, who would like to come for two nights between Sept 26th & Oct 5th, so we have looked at our dates again – we have 2 guests on October 5th, & Miss Poore could probably drive you down on 28th & you could get back to London on October 4th, & travel back on the 5th – is this possible? I know Jessie would be very disappointed not to see you – but I hope this notice is not too short. We got here Monday – my car failed on the motorway & is off for a week at least. I have Trust meetings in York, the weekend of September 14th so could you let me know HERE if possible by return, to catch me before I leave?

Jean R.

From: Whole Farm, Stone-in-Oxney, Kent. 17 September 1976.
This is one of the houses we never went to with you, I think? [Batemans, Burwash, Sussex. Rudyard Kipling's home from 1902-36, now a National Trust property] *We must try and do it next time you come here. It is a lovely place, where Kipling wrote most of his books.*

I am writing now to say that, unless you hear to the contrary, Miss Poore & I will call for you on Saturday afternoon – could you be ready about 2 o'clock? Then I thought we could drive to Whitby for some fish for our meal from the pier, have a look at the sea, & come back by Rosedale & Lastingham. It is a beautiful drive. If you want to make any alterations, I shall be at BRANDSBY 229 by Friday evening – I am not sure how long the Trust will go on, but I ought to be back by 6 o'clock. Bring old clothes – we might pick blackberries! & let us hope for good weather. Looking forward to seeing you.

Jean R.

From: Whole Farm, Stone-in-Oxney, Kent. 20 September 1976.
This is just a note to let you know that we shall be coming to the cottage at the end of next week, when I have a Trust meeting in York, & wondered if – weather permitting – you would like to come for a picnic with us on September 29 – or 30 (Wed or Thurs)? We thought of going up the coast, & having a picnic near Boggle Hole & tea in Whitby. We shall be at the cottage from Sept 24 on, so it would be safer to write there – we are well, but I have cracked a joint & have frozen shoulder. Am spending HOURS at the physiotherapist. However we have had good rainings, so no more watering is needed & the garden is looking to itself again.

Jean R.

From: Borrowdale, Cumbria. 6 October 1976[?].
We got home safely last week, but had to turn back twice to find
another route because of floods. Several cars were stuck in water and
abandoned. I have enjoyed reading the scrapbook – it is really your
family scrapbook as well as your Granny's & I think I ought to post
it back to you when I get back to the cottage – you won't want to be
without it till January. We had a lovely drive here on Monday –
sunny all the way to Kirkby Stephen, when it clouded over & got wet.
We came by Swaledale, which we didn't know, & thought it was one
of the most beautiful of the dales; quite unspoilt country. Yesterday we
got up to the top of a pass in fine weather. Then it came on to rain &
we had to come down & dry up. We did enjoy seeing you last week.

Best wishes, Jean R.

From: Whole Farm, Stone-in-Oxney, Kent. 8 October [?].
You will remember seeing this garden? [Sissinghurst Castle] This is
just to say that I have heard from Dr Goulder, who says you can't get
treatment at the hospital & have to have it done privately. Let him
know (or rather, let me know) & he will write a letter for you to give
to the physiotherapist. I hope you had a lovely time in Harrogate. I
wonder if you got to Haworth? I had the beautiful September weather
here.

All good wishes, Jean R.

From: 30 Glebe Place, Chelsea, London SW3. [?]
Thank you for such a nice letter & your sympathy over my horrid
burglary. The mess was awful – This is the only one where they took
everything of antique value as well as precious things of no value. I
am so sorry you have been feeling your illnesses so much more this
winter & it must be depressing. I do hope some more physiotherapy
may help. It will be lovely your coming in the summer with your
brother. I was down [in Kent] for 2 nights last weekend & the place
was lovely in spring flowers & the woods full of promises. Jean & Ben
are were well – I was sorry about Jemi too, but she seems to be going
on well. The quack told me she has been very ill with heart trouble –
she is better but must rest a lot & must not garden any more.

Mammie P[oore?]

From: 30 Glebe Place, Chelsea, London SW3. [?]
I am looking forward to seeing you on Thursday. If you let me know
the time you arrive I will arrange for a car to meet you at Kings

Cross. I think Amy may like to come and meet you. I unfortunately teach until 4, but hope to be free by the time you get to Glebe Place. I shan't be able to drive you down on Friday but will see that you are taken to the station on Friday afternoon. This will give you a morning to look at Chelsea antique shops, & we can arrange about a theatre for the following Thursday night – which I shall look forward to – with love Mammie Poore. PS I am afriad I have not left you much time to reply, so I suggest that we meet at 3.34 at Kings X leaving Scarboro' 10.50, unless you let me know to the contrary.

Jean R.

From: Whole Farm, Stone-in-Oxney, Kent. 5 February 1977[?].
I have just got your letter & want to get this off at once, so I haven't time to go to look at gas stoves, but Miss Poore has just arrived – (she has a nasty chest cold, & has come here for four days to be looked after & keep warm). She says she thinks you ought to ask at the Gas Showrooms for a stove which also has a CONVECTOR, as this spreads the heat more evenly all over the room. I hope they will put it in quickly – (then of course the weather will change). We must have a picnic on the cliffs next time you come. I am so glad Henry's ulcer is better – he must take care not to go too long without food. It is enough if you just suck a Horlick's milk tablet (my doctor gave me them). I have never heard of anyone going to Turkey for a week – how do people get about now!

Jean R.

From: Whole Farm, Stone-in-Oxney, Kent. 12 February 1977[?].
Thank you so much for your letter and for sending the illustration. Let me know if you want it back. It is so long since I bought a gas fire (at £5!) that I had forgotten how expensive they would be - I wanted to get something to you quickly, and didn't have a chance to ask at a shop. So here is the [ ] which I hope is right – I do want to give you the whole thing because, with everything costing so much, it is quite a big item. It looks just like the kind I hoped you would get, as it heats the whole room, not just a bit of it. It is more like spring here – tea by daylight, snowdrops & crocusses out. We have Anthea's daughter [Jean Rowntree's sisters' child] coming for the weekend, & Con [Jean R's sister] the week after.

All good wishes, Jean R.

From: Whole Farm, Stone-in-Oxney, Kent. 15 February 1977[?].
We were so glad to hear from you. I had been meaning to write to say

we had to put off coming to Brandsby. No, we are not flooded – this house, of course, is on a ridge, & the river below has been well drained lately. There were floods on some roads, but they have gone more or less now; but we did have tremendous gales – my gardening basket was blown away & I nearly went with it.

I had hoped to get to Brandsby this month or last, but my ill friend is still living, though getting weaker every day, & she does so love having short visits, and I can still go over (120 miles both ways) for 15 minutes once a week, & I can still get the peaches – at a price. Also Tony badly needs a rest & may come here if Sarah [Jean R's niece] can get away to look after Mammie – we don't know when this will be, because Sarah's matron has walked out, & they have a flu epidemic! So it doesn't look as if we could leave until April. We will certainly go then, if there is any petrol by that time. I will let you know.

Figure 18. Florence 'Milly' Kidd daughter of Edwin and Louisa Kidd.

Best wishes, Jean R.

By early to mid-1978, Milly Kidd was a permanent resident at Ravensworth Lodge, Scarborough, where she remained until her death in 1979. The staff recall Florence as a kindly, generous person and remember her with affection (Figure 18). Her obituary in the Scarborough Evening News was brief and read:

On November 30, 1979, in hospital, Florence Mildred Kidd, aged 78 years (late of 33 North Street and Ravensworth Lodge) greatly loved sister of Henry Kidd and dear aunt of Margaret and David. Service at St Laurence" church, Scalby, on Thursday (6 December) at 11.15am followed by private cremation.

With the death of Milly, the little album, so lovingly filled by three generations of the Kidd family, appears to have ceased. However, among the pages, further to those family references previously mentioned, are many others – wedding and birth notices, celebration pieces, and more obituaries to various members of the Kidd family and those related, many of whom would no doubt be familiar to residents in Scalby and include the names of Thomas Harland (of North Ferriby) brother-in-law of Milly's mother; Mrs E Tindall (of *Home Farm,* Scalby) Milly's aunt; Thomas Fenwick (of *The Park,*

Figure 19. Yew Court Terrace fronting the High Street and built by Mr Tingle Brown of Yew Court. At one time the Blacksmith had his forge in one of the properties.

Scalby); Mrs Mary Jane Kershaw (of Burniston) sister and brother-in-law of Mr and Mrs Edwin Kidd; Mr Fred Willings (of Newby) Milly's uncle; and mention is made of a Mr Crawford, a former Mayor of Scarborough in the 1940s who was best man at the wedding of Milly's parents Edwin and Hannah Kidd.

Acknowledgements

The author would like to thank Sutton Publishing for allowing the above to be taken from the book *Village Tales – The Story of Scalby and its Residents* by Alan Whitworth (1993).

Notes and References

1. Miss Jean Rowntree kept a cottage at Home Farm, Brandsby, near Hovingham, North Yorkshire.
2. Cole, John, *Historical Sketches of Scalby,* Burniston & Cloughton. 1829.
3. *ibid.*
4. *Victoria County History,* North Riding, Vol.2. 1914.
5. Bulmer's *History & Directory of North Yorkshire,* 1890.
6. Kelly's *Post Office Directory.* 1857.
7. Whellan & Co., *North Riding of Yorkshire Directory.* 1859.
9. Baine's *Yorkshire Directory* (Vol.II. North & East Riding), 1823.
10. White, William, *Yorkshire Directory,* 1840.

11. VICTORIAN WHITBY

by Dr Andrew White

BEFORE THE VICTORIAN PERIOD Whitby was principally a seaport which also attracted occasional visitors (Figure 1). From just prior to 1850 it began to develop as a seaside resort, having the added attraction of a bustling harbour (Figure 2). This change in the relative economic importance of its function occurred quite suddenly and deliberately as the result of the sale of Whitby's curious and, by the 1840s, outmoded, horse-drawn railway line to George Hudson's York and North Midland Railway Company and the subsequent creation of a link to York and beyond for steam-drawn trains. Since this change was sudden, dramatic and different in many respects from the chain of events which led to the creation of other seaside resorts[1] it is instructive to look at it in detail.

By the end of the eighteenth century Whitby was a prosperous town of just over 10,000 inhabitants, living in a few streets close to the all-important harbour, mostly

Figure 1. Whitby upper harbour in the early nineteenth century.

employed in one of the small number of staple industries such as shipbuilding and allied trades, alum-making, the Greenland whale-fishery and ship owning.[2] In terms of shipbuilding it produced the third greatest tonnage of any port in England in 1790-91 and had risen to second place in 1792-93, a truly amazing feat for a town of its size.[3] This was not maintained, and despite a revival in trade in 1838 after a slump it never reached the same significance again.

There had been considerable expansion in the area of the town in the late-eighteenth and early-nineteenth centuries with the development of *Farndale Fields*, St Hilda's Terrace and Bagdale. This was due to a very large increase in the population between 1776 and 1816, according to the historian of Whitby, George Young, writing in

Figure 2. West Cliff Estate in the late nineteenth century

1817, and to a considerable increase in wealth and prosperity partly due to government hiring of Whitby ships as 'transports' in both the Seven Years War and the Napoleonic Wars.[4] Between 1820 and 1849 there was no physical expansion at all; no new streets were built and the only new houses were rebuildings within existing streets. A number of hotels and inns existed in Whitby in the early-nineteenth century but catering for visitors was not carried out on a significant scale. Unlike its big neighbour Scarborough, it had no long tradition of catering for visitors. Scarborough's spa and sea-bathing were important as early as the beginning of the seventeenth century.[5] Further up the coast Redcar was already 'a place of fashionable resort for sea-bathing' in the early-nineteenth century.[6]

There had been much talk in Whitby in the years after 1815 about the possibility of attracting visitors to stay by the building of lodging houses. The *Whitby Magazine* commented:

> *Several families have... been obliged to leave the place in consequence of the want of sufficiently large and commodious Lodging Houses, to the very great loss of the Town and neighbourhood. We rejoice, however, to hear that in order to remedy this disadvantage, a plan for building a few respectable Lodging Houses is in a state of forwardness, and will shortly be submitted to the consideration of those whom it so deeply concerns.[7]*

A further, anonymous, article appeared in the next issue which is of interest in that it specifically suggests the West Cliff as a location, but nothing seems to have come of this plan.[8] Those with wider experience recognised the dangers to Whitby of reliance upon a few vulnerable industries – whaling had its ups and downs and so did shipbuilding – but there were those who resolutely resisted change. It was on the basis of the likely profits from the carriage of goods that the strange horse-drawn railway to Pickering went ahead after 1833, not upon the chance that it would bring visitors. Indeed, George Stephenson's report to the Committee of the projected railway in 1832 on its viability makes no mention of passenger traffic at all.[9] Although the passenger traffic was far more significant than its projectors had anticipated, the capacity of the system was too small to make much difference to the visitor population, which remained, as far as we can ascertain in the absence of a local newspaper, small and generally well-to-do; in this it mirrored the effect of road coaches rather than that of the democratising steam railways. However, it did put Whitby in somewhat easier touch with the interior and brought to the town such persons as Charles Dickens, who came in 1844 and recalled some seventeen years later his experience of the railway :

> *'In my time that curious railroad by the Whitby moor was so much the more curious, that you were balanced against a counterweight of water, and that you did it like Blondin. But in those days the one Inn of Whitby was up a back yard, and oyster-shell grottos were the only view from the best private room'.*[10]

There was a feeling in some quarters that bringing in numbers of visitors, however, respectable, would drive away the few high-spending ones who currently patronised its inns and hotels. An anonymous correspondent is quoted by Percy Shaw Jeffrey reflecting on this subject when he referred to Whitby in the year 1837 and following :

> *'I remember old Sir George Cholmondeley (sic) telling me once in the old churchyard "They had a good fishing fleet and starved it; they had a good jet trade and ruined it with foreign imitations; they had a fine lot of wealthy visitors and they'll drive the whole lot away with their constant meddling with them and what they call catering for them'*[11]

Such reactionary sentiments confused cause and effect and simply ignored the nation-wide pressures which were already affecting the fishing, particularly for herring, through the influx of Scottish and Cornish boats, the European-wide pressure from cheap jet substitutes that were competing with the jet trade, and the impact which the coming railways might have on the visitor pattern whether 'they' wanted it or not.

Despite these misgivings a Whitby Building Company was launched in 1843. It printed a prospectus for the buying of land on the West Cliff, where a large estate belonging to the Rudyard family was available, and set about erecting fourteen lodging houses there to the design of G. Matthew, of Whitby.[12] It is not clear whether this company had actually achieved anything before 1845. The probability is that it had not. In that year, George Hudson's York and North Railway acquired the railway line and within two years had re-routed it to allow steam working throughout its length (Figure 3). Hudson had either heard and approved of the lodging house idea or else it occurred to him separately – most probably the former, for he had little experience in building development – and he saw a marvellous opportunity for revitalising Whitby and giving his through-railway line a source of business at the same time. It is likely that he also saw the possibility of making himself indispensable to the electorate of Whitby, who would in consequence, make him their Member of Parliament! In the event he was offered and won the seat of Sunderland first.[13]

Figure 3. Constructing the railway into Whitby; a scene during the building of the Larpool Viaduct, c.1886

The West Cliff Estate offered some forty acres of open land close to the town centre. With the exception of *Cliff Cottage* and a few minor agricultural buildings it had never previously been built upon because the fishing and port community kept to the shelter of the harbour and the lower slopes of the cliffs, rather than risking the exposed position on the plateau above. Here was a splendid opportunity for a grand scheme, if anyone had the cash and the courage to take it. Hudson was not short of either and seized this opportunity in 1848, at first representing the York and North Midland Railway Company, but later it seems on his own behalf.[14]

First, someone with the necessary skills had to be appointed to lay out and design this grand project, which had, and has, such a key role in the appearance of the town. The architect chosen was John Dobson, who had already proved himself in Newcastle and was the creator of the style later known as 'Tyneside Classical'.[15] He handled this superb site sympathetically. His buildings were monumental and full of *gravitas* but because of their classical inspiration they were also simple and not overbearing. The choice of Dobson may have been to placate possible opponents of the scheme, although from what little we know of public opinion at that time there seems to have been few critics.

It is not clear just which buildings Dobson designed himself, other than the first blocks forming the *Royal Hotel*, East Terrace and East Crescent and also perhaps the eastern part of *Royal Crescent*. He was certainly responsible for the layout of the West Cliff Estate, including a number of features that remained unbuilt, but other architects were involved in elements of the project. Of these we know of only one by name, Henry Walker, who combined his profession with managing the *West Cliff Saloon* after it was completed. Walker had links with Sir George Elliot, magistrate and MP, who acquired the West Cliff Estate after Hudson's disgrace and he may have acted as Elliot's estates surveyor.[16] Dobson had the surface of the cliff levelled and then laid out the building sites, which from the first included ornamental flower beds to the northern side. He also had the cliff cut away to provide a sweeping roadway to approach the new development from the harbourside, with gardens and serpentine walks on its shallower eastern slopes.[17] This new approach was named 'the Khyber Pass', reflecting current British interest in affairs on the North-West Frontier of India, and it left isolated towards the harbourside a tall cragg, originally known as *Burtree Cragg* but later in another topical allusion to the South African 'Boer War' was renamed 'Spion Kop', which became a natural viewpoint over the harbour.

Figure 4. Front entrance to the *Royal Hotel* on the West Cliff

We can chart the beginning of the West Cliff development with some accuracy from two sources. The Ordnance Survey map of 1852, surveyed at the large scale of sixty inches to the mile, shows the *Royal Hotel* (first managed by Hudson's brother, Charles)(Figure 4), East Terrace, North Terrace and the West Terrace, all complete, although there is a gap where South Terrace was to stand. Since the map was actually surveyed in 1849 and there is no evidence of any revision we can assume that it records the situation up to the year 1849. All this work was that of Hudson and his architect Dobson. At this stage work had not begun on East Crescent and indeed the site is shown on the 1852 map as occupied by *Cliff Cottage*. In 1852 the *Illustrated London News* carried an engraving of 'Whitby, Yorkshire, with the recent improvements'(Figure 5). These include east Terrace with the *Royal Hotel*, and East Crescent, but in the background are other terraces of noble buildings, stretching far along the cliff. These, however, can be nothing more than figments of the artist's imagination. The accompanying text states:

'*on the west cliff, New Whitby, a magnificent pile of buildings, including a splendid hotel, recently built, containing warm baths, and every convenience for the accommodation of visitors, is admirably situated at an elevation of 100 feet above the level of the sea, commanding varied prospects, and at the same time accessible from the sands and the piers.*'

Figure 5. 'Whitby, Yorkshire - With the Recent Improvements, 1852.

Alfred, later Lord, Tennyson was in Whitby on 8 July 1852. He wrote in a letter on that day:

> *it is rather* [a] *fine place, a river running into the sea between precipices, on one side new buildings and a very handsome royal hotel belonging to Hudson the railway king, on the other at the very top a gaunt old abbey...* [18]

By 1854 Slater's *Directory* listed Belle Vue Terrace, Wellington Place and George Street (the former name for the north-south spinal road now Mulgrave Place, Havelock Place, the Esplanade, and West Terrace) so the next block of buildings to the south, behind East Crescent, was by now in occupation. On 6 July 1854 the first issue of the *Whitby Gazette* appeared in print. This was not as yet a newspaper but was instead subtitled 'Horne's List of Visitors', and gave the following locations for lodgings: East, North, South and West Terrace, (East) Crescent, Crescent Place, Wellington Place and Belle Vue Terrace, as well as a few locations in the older streets. The number of beds, sitting rooms and kitchens was listed and it is clear that even at this date the West Cliff development had added 384 bed-spaces to the accommodation of the town, exclusive of the *Royal Hotel*. The first list of visitors included a satisfactory clutch of Reverends, a doctor or two, a military title and a number of addresses containing the magical words 'Hall' or 'Park'. There were no famous names but all were eminently 'respectable', exactly the sort persons required to reassure prospective visitors that they would be in good company.

In 1859 an anonymous writer[19] could refer to a 'Company... being formed to erect a handsome Crescent. Land has been laid out for sites, roads and ornamental grounds. Several other speculators are erecting houses and terraces there.' John Dobson appears to have been responsible for the layout of the new (Royal) Crescent, which lies to the west of the earlier terraces, and his plan, dated 1859, survives in Whitby Museum. By this period, however, George Hudson was bankrupt, disgraced and living in exile in France. Despite his downfall the townsfolk continued to think kindly of Hudson and Whitby's Hudson Street retained its name, unlike the one in York which had to wait over a century for its reputation to be rehabilitated.

It is unlikely that Dobson himself had much further contact with the project after this time, though he may have designed the buildings occupying the eastern half of Royal Crescent (Figure 6). This is referred to in 1860 as 'A splendid Crescent, the radius of

Figure 6. Temperance Fete Parade in Royal Cresent on 16 August 1898.

which is about 300 feet [and] has been staked out, to be formed of 32 houses.' By the summer of 1859 the first half of the Crescent was not yet complete. Prospects for further development must have looked good in that year, for at that date the North Yorkshire and Cleveland Railway was begun, joining the Whitby and Pickering Railway at Grosmont and providing a link between Whitby and the growing industrial region of Cleveland and Durham via the Esk Valley.[20] It was more than twenty years before Whitby had a direct line via the coast, but at least it was now served by lines from both the north and south-west.

Meanwhile other building work had been going on. Further back from the cliff John Street and Hudson Street with their respective terraces of Abbey Terrace and Normanby Terrace had been taking shape. Mrs Gaskell came to stay at 1 Abbey Terrace in 1859, in order to carry out research for her novel *Sylvia's Lovers* (Figure 7).[21] She was one of the earliest visitors to lodge there. Many other literary figures followed, principally staying on the West Cliff. Most came for the picturesque townscape and the charm of the nearby moors but a more complex web of personal connections and recommendations can also be recognised. The literary and artistic 'set' of late Victorian England was not unduly large, so it is not surprising to find Sir Edward Burne-Jones' family, George Eliot, George

Figure 7. No.1 Abbey Terrace where Mrs Gaskell stayed.

Figure 8. A moving mechanical model of a Whitby Jet Works made of jet dating from the nineteenth century.

du Maurier and the Americans James Ruseel Lowell and Henry James all staying in town and all on familiar terms with one another.

Among the visitors in 1883 was George Eaton, from Norwich, who arrived with here with his family in June at the start of his month's holiday and stayed at 6 South Terrace. He paid thirty-five shillings each week for a sitting room and two bedrooms. His account of that holiday makes fascinating reading (see *Aspects of the Yorkshire Coast I*); he did all the things that a well-informed visitor was enjoined to do in Whitby, such as walking on the moors to see the ancient tumult of Swarthowe, visiting the waterfalls at Goathland or the woods at Arncliffe, travelling to Robin Hood's Bay by 'machine' and Scarborough by paddle-steamer, with longer trips by train to Rievaulx and Fountains Abbeys.[22]

Whitby itself had limited facilities for entertaining visitors

Figure 9. Selection of nineteenth century jet ornaments.

Figure 10. The West Cliff Saloon from a nineteenth century advertisement.

compared with Scarborough. It made the most of its natural advantages, however, such as its bathing beach served by bathing-machines made familiar by George du Maurier's cartoons. Walks along the two piers which, before the building of their extensions in 1914, were much more exposed to the breaking seas in stormy weather, and the cliff-top and moorland walks. By the end of the century boarding-houses were advertising the availability of tennis courts and golf links.[23] There were also the fishermen to be watched in their picturesque oilskins and sou'westers, and their stentorian wives, hawking the daily catch on the fish quay, again depicted by the pen of du Maurier.

A visit to the jet workshops was also a unique experience that Whitby could offer. George Eaton made two such visits during his holiday in 1883. Of the first he recorded, 'In the afternoon we went into some jet shops and into a workshop where two men were making jet ornaments (Figure 8 & 9). It is very dirty work. The younger of

the two was copying a head using a sharp knife for cutting the jet, which he did by eye...' There was also the Spa, then known as the West Cliff Saloon (Figure 10). Eaton thought this but a faint reflection of Scarborough's Spa. James Russell Lowell described it in 1889:

...One other amusement is the Spa, where there is a band of music bad enough to please the Shah.[25] It is brilliantly lighted and at night it is entertaining to sit above

Figure 11. No 9. Broomfield Terrace, Bagdale, one of a large Victorian terrace in which the Du Maurier family often stayed on their visits to Whitby

and watch the fashionable world laboriously diverting themselves by promenading to and fro in groups, like a village festival at the opera. The sea, of course, is as fine and irreconcilable as ever. Thank God, they can't landscape him...[26]

It is unclear at present to what extent visitors stayed for a month's holiday as opposed to shorter periods and whether they returned again and again to the same lodgings. Some of the literary and artistic families clearly stayed for a month and indeed made their holidays coincide with others in order to go for picnics and other outings together. The du Maurier family came in 1864, 1881-3, 1887, 1890-4 and 1896, staying at first at 1 St Hilda's Terrace but later at 9 Broomfield Terrace, Bagdale (Figure 11). James Russell Lowell the American poet and essayist was appointed the American Minister to the Court of St James in 1880, this appointment coincided with Lowell's first visit to Whitby in that year, and from 1880 to 1889 he spent a month or six week's here every year successively (Figure 12). These probably represent the most faithful end of the scale of

Figure 12. Bakehouse Yard, which was familiar to James Russell Lowell, who described it to a friend in a letter.

visitors, though even then the du Mauriers went in many intervening years to Dieppe.[27] By contrast, George Eaton and his family came only once, in 1883. Between 1848 and 1895 he and his family enjoyed annual holidays in many parts of the country, from Cornwall to Scotland. Eighteen of his holiday journals have survived to form a significant record of Victorian travel and leisure.[28]

The new streets of the West Cliff consisted mainly of lodging houses but significantly there was also a number of private houses.

Figure 13. Royal Cresent, Whitby, an engraving by Rock & Co. of London, showing how the Royal Cresent was to look when completed.

Figure 14. Sir George Elliott's house on the corner of the Royal Cresent and Cresent Avenue, now the *West Cliff* Hotel and other properties.

The area had started to become residential as well as providing accommodation for visitors. A Freemason's Hall was built in John Street in 1858, designed by Dobson and built by William Falkingbridge.[29] A series of prints issued by Rock and Company, of Edinburgh and others, mostly derived from drawings by the Whitby artist George Weatherill, show the new lodging houses and various prospects of the West Cliff (Figure 13). Some include elements as yet unbuilt at that date, and never to be erected, which lessens their usefulness as a historical document but serves to show the pride with which Whitby greeted its new developments.

In retrospect we can see that the period 1849 to 1860 as the high-watermark of the West Cliff development. Sir George Elliot had taken over Hudson's interests in the scheme but his own house, the curious neo-Baroque structure on the unfinished side of the Crescent (Figure 14), designed for him by Henry Walker in about 1860,[30] seems to mark the point at which the impetus went out of the whole project. Indeed, the fact that this rather exuberant house does not match the rather sober elevations of the eastern half of the Crescent and would not have allowed the degree of symmetry originally proposed suggests that the scheme was already in difficulties. Work went on in a desultory fashion creating further streets. We can chart the progress through trade directories. The Esplanade had appeared by 1879 along with (Royal) Crescent Avenue.[31] By 1890 Church Square, facing St Hilda's Church, and Langdale Terrace were in existence.[32] Much further along the cliff

Figure 15. *Lorne Villas* on the edge of the West Cliffe Estate facing towards the West Cliff Railway Station.

Lorne Villas had appeared by 1879 (Figure 15), Argyle Road and Ocean Road by 1899 and the monumentally ugly *Metropole Hotel* in 1897-8, to the design of Chorley, Cannon and Chorley of Leeds.[33] These developments were unrelated to the original West Cliff Estate and had much more to do with the opening in 1883 of the Whitby, Redcar and Middlesbrough Union Railway, that ran along the high cliffs of Cleveland in a most picturesque fashion. This line was provided with a new West Cliff station off Upgang Road 'erected specially for the residents and visitors in that fashionable locality'. Construction of the railroad began as early as 1871 but due to engineering difficulties and bad workmanship by the first contractor it took twelve years to complete.[34]

Figure 16. A map of Whitby showing the proposed layout much of which was never completed.

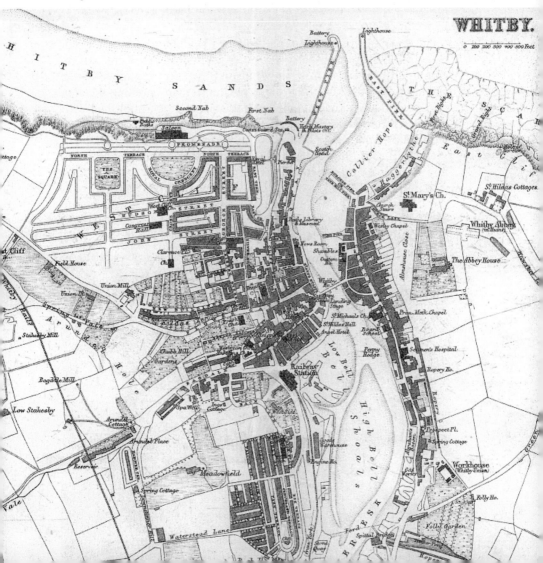

Figure 17. A view across the harbour to Fishburn Park estate. Many of the houses here were built of white brick, known locally as 'ballast bricks' and often brought to the town in the bottom of ships as ballast.

An undated map, on internal evidence belonging to about 1860, shows what might have been (Figure 16). A series of projected streets continues from John Street and Hudson Street crossing other streets leading to a square on the Promenade, more than doubling the area of development actually completed. A map of 1895, published with the fourth edition of Horne's *Guide to Whitby* illustrates the situation at the end of the century, when it was clear that the grand scheme of the 1850s would never be accomplished. Tennis courts and gardens now occupy the areas where fashionable lodging houses were to have stood and Whitby had to wait for another burst of building activity in the 1930s for a thin straggle of hotels and private houses to line the cliff west of the Spa.[35]

While the West Cliff underwent its high-profile development, the

Figure 18. *Fairmead,* formerly the home of a member of the ship building family of Turnbull, now demolished.

rest of the town did not stand still. Shortly after the West Cliff works began, in 1853, land consisting of three fields off Waterstead Lane and Bog Hall was put up for sale, close to the western side of the upper harbour.[36] Building started shortly afterwards and resulted in two main types of house. The first to be erected were terraces of large lodging houses on the lower slopes, overlooking the harbour. These were Esk Terrace, Cleveland Terrace and parts of Park Terrace, which all appeared in White's *Directory* for 1858. Later a number of streets containing both large and small dwelling houses took shape further up the hill, in the second field. These included Scoresby Terrace and Oswy Street by 1864, Falcon Terrace, Elgin Street, Gray Street, Grove Street and Raglan Terrace by 1879, Osborne Terrace by 1890 and Hope Terrace by 1899.

It might be thought that these houses were built to accommodate those employed in looking after the visitors but in fact they appear to have been occupied by people involved in a wider variety of work. Despite their small size even some of the houses in Scoresby Terrace were listed as 'lodging-houses', while others were occupied by small tradesmen, such as butchers, joiners and boot and shoe makers. The slightly larger houses attracted another group of occupants. In 1890 my great-grandfather and three of his brothers, all of them master mariners lived in Elgin Street and York Place, while another great-grandfather, also a master mariner, lived close by in Falcon Terrace.[37] people made frequent moves between these streets, usually to larger houses with room for growing families, because they were mainly renting property. The whole development, known at first as 'Meadowfield Park' and later as 'Fishburn Park', is now known universally as 'The Railway' because of its position overlooking the station (Figure 17). No doubt the proximity of the railway station was also a significant factor in building a number of lodging houses here, since most visitors to Whitby came by train and sought to carry their luggage the shortest possible distance.

Figure 19. Detail of the house name *Fairmead*. Many Victorian houses in the town have exquisite terracotta details like this.

Other houses were being constructed elsewhere. Hanover Terrace, on the western side of Downdinner Hill, appeared before 1864.[38] Broomfield Terrace, a row of ten large white-brick lodging houses designed by Noel Armfield, in Bagdale, was there by 1879.[39] These houses back on to the earlier *Victoria or Bagdale Spa*; the little conical-roofed well-house of this Spa still survives. Its water was compared with that of Tunbridge Wells for is medicinal properties and season tickets for it could be obtained in 1860 from the proprietor John Stevenson.[40] Other large and ugly brick lodging houses colonised the slopes of upper Bagdale and Chubb Hill towards the close of the century,and some of the latter houses may have been dwelling houses from the beginning. So the capacity for accommodating visitors on the west side of the town increased markedly in the second half of the nineteenth century and was matched by a demand for large family houses for those successful middle-class families who had prospered from Whitby's trades, in particular master mariners and shipowners, the two often being synonymous (Figure 18 & 19). It is not always easy to distinguish lodging houses from large family houses designed to be run by a large staff of servants.

A relatively large and rapid development such as the West Cliff Estate left, not surprisingly, a record in the large number of artisans involved in its construction. The 1851 Census Enumerators' return records the following builders: George Vasey, of Church Street, with eight employees; William Langdale, of Baxtergate, with thirty men, and John Bolton, of Flowergate with twenty-seven men. The latter was probably the son of John Bolton, the builder of the Baths,

Library and Museum building in 1827 near Haggersgate and other later Georgian buildings[41] who had already made a significant contribution to the townscape. In addition there were twenty-six bricklayers and labourers, seventy stonemasons, thirty-two joiners and house carpenters, six plasterers and ten others, totalling 245 men, for whom no employer is given. In his analysis of this census Rodway states that as no building works are listed, most of these men must have worked outside the town or on non public

Figure 20. A nineteenth century drawing of Trinity Presbyterian Church, Whitby.

buildings. However, Victorian builders took on workers for specific projects and would not have kept them on the payroll in times of depression in the trade.[42] This uncommonly large workforce can hardly have been assembled for other than a major development such as Hudson's West Cliff works. The Census Enumerators' Return made no mention of the West Cliff probably because it did not as yet represent occupied houses. Three brick-makers also operated on the west side of Whitby. The source of any locally-made bricks in the eighteenth century buildings of the town is unknown but in 1854 William Thompson, brick-maker, is listed in the trade directory on the West Cliff.[43] His brickworks lay to the north of the development, in the area later occupied by tennis courts and putting greens.

Figure 21. The Brunswick Wesleyan Church, Whitby.

It is somewhat surprising to find that no specific provision was made for any churches in the new West Cliff development. The Victorian age tended towards an over-provision of churches if anything and Whitby was generally well-provided. The two new Anglican churches of the late 1840s were St John's, in Baxtergate, and St Michael's, in lower

Figure 22. A representation of the burning of Whitby Theatre in 1823. This stood in what is now Brunswick Street opposite the Brunswick Church.

Church Street, neither of them related to the activities on the West Cliff.[44] Two Nonconformist churches, Trinity Presbyterian church (Figure 20), in Flowergate, of 1877-8, and the Congregational church at the upper end of Skinner Street, of 1868, may have served some parts of the West Cliff population.[45] It was not until 1868 that the so-called 'Iron Church' was put up, eventually to be replaced by the present St Hilda's Church close by in a prominent position at the top of Hudson Street in 1884-6, well after the impetus had gone out of the development. St Hilda's is a big church, designed for the peculiar circumstances of the seaside, with aisles which could absorb the summer overflow and be closed off in winter when the congregation dwindled. The church was financed by public subscription, although Sir George Elliot gave the site and some money, the York Diocesan Church Building Society gave £400 and the family of the Reverend John Turner, a former curate, gave a further £4,200 to complete it.[46]

One reason for the lack of early church provision may be the way in which the parish church dominated affairs in Whitby. There was, and still is, only one parish in Whitby. All the Anglican churches were no more than chapels-of-ease to St Mary, served by the Rector and his band of curates. Rectors in the nineteenth century included some powerful and uncompromising men such as Canon George Austen (Rector 1875-1924) who were unlikely to allow the parish and its revenues to be diminished by carving out new parishes within it. The population of Whitby was little more than 12,000 in the mid-nineteenth century and was moreover very densely packed into a small area. The parish church was inconveniently placed on top of the cliff, with no houses close by, but for all the main life-events of its parishioners including funerals, there was no alternative but attendance there.[47] For funerals it was somewhat problematical, but for visitors its position was a decided attraction. One visitor in 1835, Sir George Head, was moved to this description of the stairs leading up from the town to St Mary's:

> *These steps may be seen every Sunday covered from top to bottom with old and young, - parents at the decline of life, children at its commencement, - both together surmounting the arduous ascent, and wending their way to the sacred edifice . . . I was forcibly reminded, on such an occasion, of Bunyan's beautiful allegory of 'The Hill of Difficulty.*[48]

It is clear that many holiday-makers must have spread their attendance around the various churches. The Victorian Sunday was a

Figure 23. A nineteenth century Du Maurier cartoon from Punch, 10 September 1887.

serious matter and church attendance not to be shirked, especially when on holiday. Different churches in Whitby might be visited for Matins and Evensong by visiting Anglicans, while those who wished to take long perambulations were positively encouraged by local guidebooks to use neighbouring churches such as those at Ruswarp and Ugglebarnby, as a strategic point to break their Sunday walks. 'Service at Ugglebarnby Church would perhaps best divide this somewhat long distance', was recommended by the 1895 Horne's Guide. George Eaton and his family attended services at all the Anglican churches of the town during their month's holiday in 1883:

Figure 24. An aerial photoghraph of the West Cliff Estate and the Royal Cresent, Whitby, taken before 1926.

Figure 25. A typical Victorian house interior of the wealthy middle class, in this instance *Bagdale Hall,* now a hotel, and one of the oldest buildings in the town.

StNinian's and St Michael's on 24 June; the parish church and St Ninian's on 1 July; none on 8 July, due to illness; and finally St John's and the 'Iron Church' on 15 July. Eaton makes no comment on any of the services but clearly disapproves of the recent Anglo-Catholic refitting of St Ninian's, 'which has lately been done up to some very high notions'.

Whitby was redeveloped in the mid-nineteenth century as a middle-class seaside resort. Large lodging-houses catered solely for

Figure 26. Another room in *Bagdale Hall* as it was furnished in the nineteenth century.

reasonably affluent families staying mostly for the traditional month in the summer (Figure 23). A great many changes have overtaken this pattern of holiday-making, including the spread down the social scale during the late-nineteenth century and more recently the growth of the foreign holiday, and now the housing stock is no longer relevant to modern requirements. While some hotels and guest-houses do reasonably well (Figure 24). Most of the former lodging-houses are now let out all the year round as flats or, in some cases, have become self-catering holiday accommodation. Much of the latter is now provided by former fishermen's cottages in the yards and courts off Church Street, small but picturesque and thus capable of attracting those in search of something different. Thus, ironically, much of the Victorian holiday accommodation has become permanent residential stock while the former workers' housing has become the holiday accommodation of today.

Whitby was never intended as a mass holiday resort and did not even grow as far or as fast as its projectors had imagined. Nowadays much of its business is in day visitors. Many of the holiday cottages are owned by people living elsewhere, typically in West Yorkshire, so relatively little of the profits of tourism reaches the local economy although Whitby can still be a very bustling place on summer weekends with most of its services at full stretch.

Acknowledgements

I am grateful to those who have helped with material for this article. I would particularly like to thank Elisabeth Melrose at North Yorkshire County Library Service for help with Trade Directories, Mr H L Fleming at Whitby Literary & Philosophical Society, Captain T C Eaton of Norwich for allowing me to quote from his grandfather's journal and Norwich Record Office for giving me access to it. Finally to the publishers of *The Local Historian* in which magazine this article first appeared in May 1998 (Volume 28 No 2).

Notes

1. For general histories of the rise of the seaside holiday see Hern, A, *The Seaside Holiday*.
2. *The History of the English Seaside Resort* (London, 1967); Walvin, J *Beside the Seaside; a Social History of the Popular Seaside Holiday* (London, 1978); Walton, J. K & Walvin, J (eds), *Leisure in Britain, 1780-1939* (Manchester, 1983); Walton, J K, *The English Seaside Resort: A Social History 1750-1914* (Leicester, 1983). The last reference shows clearly how Whitby, twelfth largest of seventy-one resorts in 1851, its population swollen by the non-resort element, rapidly slipped down both the population table and growth table compared to other resorts. In 1911 it was thirty-sixth of a longer list in terms of population and bottom of the list for growth in the period 1881-1911.
3. White, A J, *History of Whitby* (Chichester, 1993).
4. MacGregor, D R, *Merchant Sailing Vessels: Sovereignty of Sail 1775-1815* (London,1985), pp14-22.
5. White, A J, *Buildings of Georgian Whitby* (Keele, 1995); Young, G, *A History of Whitby and*

Streonshalh Abbey (Whitby, 1817), pp514-7.

6. Edwards, M (ed), *Scarborough 966-1966* (Scarborough, 1966), p63ff.

7. Bigland, J, *The Beauties of England and Wales.* Vol.XVI Yorkshire (London, 1812), p314; Saltburn another near neighbour of Whitby was created by the Saltburn Improvement Company in 1860, somewhat later than Whitby, from a humble fishing hamlet; Lidster, J, *Yorkshire Coast Lines.*

8. *Historical Record of Railway Tourism on the Yorkshire Coast* (Nelson, 1983), p41.

9. *Whitby Magazine,* Vol.1, 1827, pp286-7.

ibid, pp306-9.

10. Quoted in Potter, G W J, *A History of the Whitby and Pickering Railway* (London, 1906), pp10-14.

11. Quoted in Whitworth, *Whitby As They Saw It* (Whitby, 1991), p34.

12. Jeffrey, Percy Shaw, *Whitby Lore and Legend* (2nd Edn, Whitby, 1923), pp272-3.

13. Peacock, J *George Hudson 1800-71; The Railway King* (London, 1988), pp463-6.

14. Lambert, R S, *The Railway King 1800-71* (London, 1949), pp272-3.

ibid, p272.

15. Wilkes, L, *John Dobson, Architect and Landscape Gardener* (Stocksfield, 1980).

16. *Whitby Official Directory,* 1899.

17. Robinson, F K, *Whitby, its Abbey and the Principal Parts of the Neighbourhood* (Whitby, 1860), p207.

18. Whitworth, *Whitby As They Saw It,* p33.

19. Whellan & Co, *History & Topography of the City of York and the North Riding of Yorkshire* (Beverley, 1859), p286.

17. Robinson, *Whitby,* pp120-1, 208.

18. Kendal, H P, *Whitby in Literature* (Whitby, nd), pp4-5.

19. Norwich Record Office, Eaton 4.2.71 VII.

20. Horne's *Guide to Whitby* (4th edn, Whitby, 1895), pp181,183.

21. 'Whitby Jottings', *Illustrated London News* (19 Oct 1889).

22. The 'Shah' was Prince Dhuleep Singh who was ousted out of India by the British and subsequently offered a home in Britain by Queen Victoria. For a period he leased Mulgrave castle nearby and was a familiar figure in the town.

23. Kendall, *Whitby in Literature,* p9.

24. Ormond, *George du Maurier* (London, 1969), p409ff, and *Punch* for the years listed.

25. Gard, R, *The Observant Traveller* (London, 1989), p116.

26. Robinson, *Whitby,* p171.

27. Pevsner, Sir Nikolaus, *The Buildings of England; North Riding of Yorkshire* (London, 1966), p399.

28. *Post Office Directory,* 1879.

29. Bulmer's *History, Topography and Directory of North Yorkshire,* 1890.

30. Pevsner, *Buildings of England.*

31. Hoole, K, *The Whitby, Redcar and Middlesbrough Union Railway* (Nelson, 1994), p4.

32. White, *History of Whitby,* p60.

34. *ibid,* fig.30.

35. *Bulmer's Directory,* 1890.

36. *Slater's Directory,* 1864.

37. *Post Office Directory,* 1879.

38. Robinson, *Whitby,* pp195-6.

39. White, *Buildings of Georgian Whitby,* p22.

40. Rodawy, E, *Whitby in 1851* (Whitby, nd), pp6-7; Higgs, E, *Making Sense of the census - the Manuscript Returns for England and Wales 1801-1901* (London, 1989); Powell, C G *An Economic*

41. *History of the British Building Industry, 1815-1979* (London, 1980).

42. *Slater's Directory, 1854-5.*

43. Whellan, *History and Topography of the City of York,* p310.

44. *Bulmer's Directory,* 1890, pp1139-40.

45. *ibid,* pp1137-8; *The Building News* (23 Oct 1885).

46. The cemetery was opened in 1862 and burials in the churchyard other than in existing graves ceased.

47. *Bulmer's Directory,* 1890, pp1140-1.

48. Head, Sir George, *A Home Tour through the Manufacturing Districts of England in the Summer of 1835* (London, 1836, reprinted 1968), p282.

CONTRIBUTORS

1. BRIDLINGTON - THE GROWTH OF A HOLIDAY RESORT

Howard Peach was born into a mining family at Selston, in Nottinghamshire in March 1932. After National Service in the RAF he trained as a teacher in Leeds, subsequently gaining London degrees in Economics and History of Education. Headships in Norfolk and Hampshire preceded his removal to Willerby in 1978. Whenever the pressures of bringing up four children allowed, he pursued his writing and research, especially in education, poetry, short stories and local history. Since retiring in 1992 he has had more time to enjoy his family, now enlarged to include four grandchildren, and to travel ever hopefully across these 'Broad Acres', taking photographs of 'curiosities' and looking for material for future books and articles.

2. WHEN ELEPHANTS ROAMED THE STREETS OF WHITBY
10. PLAIN TALES FROM SCALBY

Alan Whitworth trained at Bradford College of Art, but from 1977, after a number of years in the world of printing and graphic art, he predominately turned his attention to promoting the preservation of English parish churches, founding and running a charity to that end, writing and lecturing on the subject, mounting many exhibitions prmoting the beauty of our homeland churches and organising the first national conference dealing with churches and tourism; and yet his interests are wider, and his regard for old buildings and history has led in one area to the founding of the Yorkshire Dovecote Society after a study of dovecotes and pigeon-lofts, about which he has written and lectured often, and in another, to compile a number of visual records about places with which he has been associated. He now writes and lectures about local history subjects and his books include *Exploring Churches* (in associated 1986, 1993); *Yorkshire Windmills* (1991); *Village Tales - The Story of Scalby* (1993); *A History of Bradley* (1998) and *A Travellers Guide to the Esk Valley Railway* (1998).

3. Wells and Holy Wells of the Yorkshire Coast

Edna Whelan hails from the Brontë country, and while living in Skipton, served as a town councillor. She adores the wind-swept moors and heather, but her greatest delight is the open sea. She has an in-born love of adventure and has had – and in her seventies, is still having a full and varied life with many interests, painting, caving, studying ancient and medieval history, and latterly, sailing, to name but a few. Edna is also an authority on Holy Wells about which she has written often, and is a founder member of the Holy Wells Research and Preservation Group. Now living in Whitby, Edna met and joined in the adventures of Captain Jack Lammiman, which she shared in her book, *The Helga Maria* (Caedmon Publishers, 1992) which later formed the basis for a film about the life and voyages of Captain Jack starring Bob Hoskins and Maureen Lipman. A widow, Edna keeps in touch with her sons and daughter Cynthia who lives and teaches in Monaco, and her five grandchildren.

4. The Cloughton Whales

Ben Chapman, woodcarver, artist, poet and social history writer, was born in Kingston-upon-Hull in 1941. He has always had an interest in history, and is especially interested in the medieval period and in the eighteenth and nineteenth centuries. With his late wife Mave, he collaborated on a number of books, subjects as diverse as life in domestic service and a history of Pierrots. Ben has also made several contributions to an international heraldic dictionary and his last book is about misericord carvings in Yorkshire churches. He is currently working on a large format picture book of misericords, a volume of animal poetry and a *Dictionary of Bare Knuckle Prize-fighting*. Ben Chapman now resides in Withensea and is a member of the Withensea Writers Group.

5. The Rise and Fall of East Coast Fishing

Alma Brunton was born in Middlesbrough. During her career she has been the Manageress of a chemist in Middlesbrough, where her first husband had a senior position in the Dock Masters Office of Middlesbrough Docks. His keen interest in fishing which he passed on to their only child Reginald (Reg), provided the inspiration for Alma's own interest in the sea. Moving to Whitby over twenty-five years ago, she managed Crockett's Dry Cleaners in the town for many years until her retirement. Later after her husband died, she remarried and still lives in Whitby. Among her interests Alma lists writing, ballroom dancing in which she has gained many medals and certificates and cake decoration.

6. Andrew Marvell - Cromwell's Poet

Alexandra Heywood lives with David and son Rhys in Huddersfield, where she has been employed at a local secondary modern school for the past six years. She has a degree in Computer Studies and also gained a Certificate in Education (Cert.Ed) at Huddersfield University. Work and working with children she says, has broadened her knowledge and interests in many subjects, particularly history and literature. Alex enjoys many hobbies, but particularly likes to spend time with her family and is keen to ensure that Rhys, now aged twelve years, enjoys and benefits from a good academic and sports education.

7. Curiosities of the Yorkshire Coast

Eileen Rennison was born in 1927 in a North Riding village and moved to York at the age of ten. Except briefly when first married she has lived all her life in Yorkshire. Educated at Mill Mount Grammar School and York School of Art, she qualified as a teacher of art at the College of Ripon and York St John and

ended her teaching career as a lecturer there. Eileen met her husband when they were both art students and they have a son in the book trade and a married daughter, a German son-in-law and two grand-daughters living in Berlin. Eileen Rennison is an author of many articles on numerous subjects and three books on the subject of the curiosities of various parts of Yorkshire under the title *In Search of the Unusual* published by Hutton Press.

---

8. The Smugglers Revenge

Peter Howorth, born a Lancastrian, settled in East Yorkshire after studying history at the University of Hull. He was awarded a Master of Philosophy degree in history for research into aspects of local history and has lectured and written widely on the subject. After teaching in schools in Beverley, Driffield and Howden, Peter now lives in Driffield, where retired he owns a small publishing company. He has written five books, including *A History of East Yorkshire Cricket 1778-1914, Crimes and Punishment in Yorkshire 1800-37* and a biography of Luke White, the first working-class Member of Parliament to represent the East Riding.

---

9. Come Rain, Come Shine - The Langtoft Floods

David Wright was born in Bridlington in 1945. After a basic education he left school in 1960 and followed various professions in his hometown until 1963, then spent four years in West London. Returning to Bridlington in 1967 he obtained a post with the then Yorkshire Electricity Board (YEB) with which he was employed for the following twenty-five years. Married in 1970, he and his wife Carole have three grown-up children. Work published over four decades includes record and book reviews, short stories, poetry, local interest articles and other offerings featured in publication's as diverse as Ludd's Mill and *Pennine Platform*. He has had seven collections of verse published over the years; the last of which was by Grafitti Petals Publications, of

Houston, Texas. David has also completed an extensive family history in 1997, and is currently working on a series of local history essays entitled, *Riding East - Tales from the Coast and Wolds.*

---

11. VICTORIAN WHITBY

Andrew White has spent over a quarter of a century working in museums and archaeology. He studied for an MA in Classics at Lancaster University and for a Ph.D in Archaeology at Nottingham University. A Fellow of the Museums Association and of the Society of Antiquaries, he is married with three children, and is presently Curator of Lancaster City Museums. In his spare time he writes, lectures and broadcasts on local history subjects. Dr White's ancestors have lived in Whitby for more than two hundred years, mostly as mariners, which probably accounts for his lifelong affection for the town and his fascination with its history.

INDEX